Praise for *The Power of Real Confidence*

Michelle is all about performance and potential and she truly understands what real confidence can do for leaders and their organisations. She connects at a deep and genuine level to help leaders unlock and discover their true confidence and this resonates throughout her book, *The Power of Real Confidence*. The fact that she is able to bring years of her own leadership experience, as well as now working with leaders across every spectrum of industry, ensures this book will hit the mark for you. It is a must-have for any leader wanting to lift their and their team's performance, confidence and impact!

Jamie McPhee, Chief Executive Officer, ME Bank

I wish I had been given a book like this years ago. Forget your ABC's, Michelle is teaching us letters for life confidence when it comes to Learn, Lead, Live or the four S's – Show Up, Stand Up, Speak Up, Step Up. Never one to shy away from reality, the section on the three P's for dealing with setbacks is critical advice. Backed up with real-life examples and compelling storytelling, *The Power of Real Confidence* is a terrific read for anyone at any stage in their career journey. As quoted in this fantastic book, we all just need to #ownit.

Jac Phillips, Senior Director, Head of Marketing,
Visa Australia, NZ and South Pacific, VISA

In her book, *The Power of Real Confidence*, Michelle Sales provides tools and seriously actionable advice for building and sustaining confidence. Michelle really gets what it takes for leaders to show up, stand up, speak up and step up with confidence. This book is a must-read for leaders at all levels.

Sue Matthews, Chief Executive Officer, The Royal Women's Hospital

Michelle Sales is on a mission to help build a society that enables individuals to confidently demonstrate leadership success without shunning the important contribution of personal attributes. This book eschews complexity in favour of a clarity of process, which in itself is almost deceptively simplistic, as it takes readers on a journey to success. Her emphasis on authenticity – be real, be yourself – strikes a chord with my own experience leading a large and complex organisation comprising myriad passionate personalities collaborating towards a single vision. With so much 'advice' on leadership, time with this book is time well spent.

Claire Spencer, Chief Executive Officer, Arts Centre Melbourne

How do we make the most of our talents, skills, and interests? How do we inspire confidence in others? How do we build and maintain it in ourselves? Michelle Sale's book, *The Power of Real Confidence*, demonstrates that it's not enough to know what we're doing; our confidence is a key factor in our leadership success. In fact, you could say that confidence is the ultimate leadership skill! With real-life stories and practical advice backed by research, you'll want this book on your shelf!

Gavin Slater, Chief Executive Officer, Digital Transformation Agency

Confidence is such an important fuel that can power you forward in whatever life adventures you choose. If you are serious about strengthening your confidence and leadership skills, in a way that is authentic and sustainable, this book has a wealth of practical tips and suggestion. I've had the privilege of working through many of these tools and exercises first-hand with Michelle, and her book effectively captures the essence of what she communicates in an accessible and impactful way.

Lynne Storey Naphtali, Commercial Director, Accenture

In *The Power of Real Confidence*, Michelle Sales takes us on an insightful discovery of how building real confidence is so powerful in reaching our leadership potential. The ability for us as leaders to recognise the role that confidence can play and how we go about building it is essential. This book belongs in the toolkit of every leader as they progress through their career!

Hilary Crowe, VP Human Resources and Communications, Amcor

Michelle is a true 'in the moment' professional whose content, insights and engagement is amazing, and this transcends into her book, *The Power of Real Confidence*. Michelle easily translates complex research into understandable, practical and vital tools essential for any leader looking to build their own (and their team's) capability and confidence.

Mike Cameron, Group Executive, Customer and Revenue, PEXA

Improving the lives of people and their organisations through great leadership isn't just a business for Michelle, it's her genuine passion. In a world where technology continues to disrupt at a pace never seen before – Michelle gives teams the tools to reach their full potential and increase performance. She is a true master at maximising leadership potential in an authentic manner.

Janelle Hopkins, Group CFO, Australia Post

...a must-read guide for leaders who want to expand their confidence. *The Power of Real Confidence* outlines a clear set of steps readers can take to build more confidence to enable them to step up and lead to their full potential. Confidence is 'learnable' and this book is full of practical tips and strategies to build and sustain leadership confidence. I couldn't put it down!

Andrea Brunner, Chief Client Officer, FMG

Picking up another book on leadership always fills me with trepidation. Will I learn something new? Hasn't it all been said before? Reading Michelle's book has left me feeling renewed and with more energy than ever before to embrace the leader I am and to continually strive to be better. I often doubt my ability and this book reminds me that I am not alone. Confidence is so important and ensuring I don't give the self-doubt in my head too much space is critical. *The Power of Real Confidence* has given me some tools that will really help me and will help the teams I lead. Thank you Michelle for sharing your wisdom and experience.

Linda Barry, General Manager Programs,
Alannah and Madeline Foundation

Confidence can come to us and leave us at any time. No-one is immune and the people who exude confidence are often working very hard to achieve it. *The Power of Real Confidence* is overflowing with practical advice, the latest research and powerful stories. Regardless of where you are in your career this book will help you Show Up, Stand Up, Speak Up and Step Up.

Gabrielle Dolan, best-selling author of *Stories for Work* and speaker on authentic communication

How do we truly maximise our leadership potential? This book demonstrates that it's not enough to just know our stuff. *The Power of Real Confidence* shows how you can move from building capability and confidence in yourself, to inspiring confidence in others, which ultimately maximises your own leadership potential.

Lee Scales, Chief Customer Officer and Executive Manager, People Services, UniSuper

THE
POWER
OF REAL
CONFIDENCE

LEARN HOW TO LEAD TO
YOUR FULL POTENTIAL

MICHELLE SALES

First published in 2018 by Major Street Publishing Pty Ltd
PO Box 106, Highett, Vic. 3190
E: info@majorstreet.com.au
W: majorstreet.com.au
M: +61 421 707 983

Ordering information

Quantity sales. Special discounts are available on quantity purchases by
corporations, associations and others. For details, contact Lesley Williams
using the contact details above.

Individual sales. Major Street publications are available through most bookstores.
They can also be ordered directly from Major Street's online bookstore at
www.majorstreet.com.au/shop.

Orders for university textbook/course adoption use. For orders of this nature,
please contact Lesley Williams using the contact details above.

The moral rights of the author have been asserted.

A catalogue record for this
book is available from the
National Library of Australia

ISBN: 978-0-6482387-9-9

Internal design by Production Works
Cover design by Simone Geary
Cover photo by Timothy Arch – Arch Creative
Printed in Australia by ☒ ☒P☒ers☒n☒ Printin☒ Gr☒u☒

10 9 8 7 6 5 4 3 2 1

Disclaimer: The material in this publication is in the nature of general comment only, and
neither purports nor intends to be advice. Readers should not act on the basis of any matter
in this publication without considering (and if appropriate taking) professional advice
with due regard to their own particular circumstances. The author and publisher expressly
disclaim all and any liability to any person, whether a purchaser of this publication or not,
in respect of anything and the consequences of anything done or omitted to be done by
any such person in reliance, whether whole or partial, upon the whole or any part of the
contents of this publication.

CONTENTS

ABOUT THE AUTHOR

Michelle Sales is passionate about helping people tap into their true potential – in leadership and in life.

As a highly sought-after speaker, trainer, facilitator and coach, she has helped thousands of senior leaders and their teams learn to show up as the best version of themselves, to build their confidence and influence with others, and to maximise their leadership and performance.

Michelle worked for 28 years in corporate roles – with many of those being senior and executive leadership roles in financial services – before establishing her own leadership business in 2012. From her experience, she understands the real challenges and opportunities that leaders in business face every day. Stepping up with real confidence takes work – both to build confidence and, more importantly, to sustain it. So the systems and processes she uses are based on real-life results and are things she practises regularly herself.

Michelle loves learning and is constantly seeking to improve her own knowledge, capability and edge in order to add value to her clients. She is currently studying positive psychology, and is a past graduate from the Harvard Kennedy School Executive Education's Art and Practice of Leadership Development and Women and Power: Leadership in a New World programs. In 2016, she was nominated for the Telstra Business Women's Awards.

Michelle is loved by her clients, colleagues and friends for her authenticity and warmth as much as for her hard-hitting ability to hold people to account.

This is her first book, but she is confident it is not her last.

To find out more about Michelle, go to michellesales.com.au.

ACKNOWLEDGEMENTS

This book was written in my head well before I ever put pen to paper. In fact, the pen-to-paper part has been my greatest challenge. (If you've ever written a book, you will know what I mean.) This struggle in itself has, at times, really affected my own confidence, and I have used many of the tools in this book to build my confidence back up and sustain me until the end of the project. Many others helped along the way too, I would like to thank some of them here.

Firstly, thanks to Kelly Irving, my brilliant developmental editor. Without her this book would still be in my head. She took my very early thoughts – what I know and what I do in my work – and helped me actually write a book. Something I still find hard to believe! Thanks to Lesley Williams and the team at Major Street Publishing. The process of writing a book is such a mystery when you start out and Lesley made it so easy. I always felt in safe hands.

Thanks also to my colleague, Gabrielle Dolan. You gave me great mentoring advice when I first started my business and then gave me the push I needed to write this book. When I need guidance or advice, you are always there for me and I so appreciate your support and friendship.

I have many brilliant and supportive colleagues who have given me a well-needed boost through the writing of this book. I work in such a supportive industry and I love it.

I would especially like to thank Kate Hughes, Cindy Batchelor and Janelle Hopkins for sharing their stories about their leadership and confidence journeys.

I also have some of the best clients around. I often find myself learning as much from them as they do from me, and I find that so rewarding. Through the process of writing this book, so many of my clients were supportive and many provided stories that helped bring my words to life. Thanks to Angela Middleton, Jac Phillips, Sarah White, Somone Johns and Jo Campbell for your long-term support of me and the work that I do. It makes such a difference knowing you are in my corner.

To my small but very special team, I could not have done this without you. Danielle Woollard, you got this off the ground! Your encouragement and early work made my start on this book an easier one. Caroline Loughrey and Maria Palazon, you are my rocks. I love our little team, and at many points along the way you have kept the business running as my head was buried in writing. Thank you.

Thanks also to Mum and Dad, for bringing me up to believe that anything is possible. That in itself gave me such a wonderful start in my own confidence journey. Your unwavering support, guidance and love have meant so much to me.

And to my very special friends who I spend so much time with – thank you for listening to my ideas and to my rants when I was just over it all, and for your loyal and lasting friendship and love. I have felt supported every step of the way.

To my gorgeous cavoodle, Molly – sure, you won't be reading this book, but you sat beside me as I wrote every single word. The walks and plays in the park that you sacrificed are much appreciated.

Finally, to you, the reader – thank you for taking the time to read my book. My hope for you is that you do more than just absorb it; I hope that you take action, try new things, open yourself up to new opportunities and challenges and, ultimately, realise your own leadership potential. And I hope you enjoy working your way through this book as much as I enjoyed writing it.

I wish you all the very best on your own confidence journey.

WHY CONFIDENCE IS CRITICAL TO LEADERSHIP SUCCESS

Do you feel like you're really great at your job but you just can't crack that promotion? Alternatively, do you ever question your ability and feel as if you haven't been able to step up your leadership? Do you ever feel exhausted from your leadership work because you're constantly trying to be something you're not?

Everyone, from those starting out in their first 'real' jobs to experienced leaders in the senior ranks of organisations, have moments – days, months, years even – when they question their ability to face challenges, and when their confidence feels threatened. You might question your own ability to have an impact and to negotiate and stand up for yourself, whether in your career, about your salary or with your clients and stakeholders.

Maybe you've been trying to break through to senior leadership levels and don't know how to do this. Your colleagues with more confidence and a stronger presence are now being promoted above you. You may be asking yourself what you need to do differently to be considered ready for promotion. *Whose support do I need? How do I develop the level of confidence and influence I will need at this level? And will I really be able to do it?*

No-one is immune to bouts of insecurity at work – but that doesn't have to hold you back. Without confidence, you can't exercise leadership with real impact, and have teams and stakeholders who believe in you and want to follow you. If you set your bar too low, you fail to maximise your potential, and the potential of your team, your business and your organisation.

Remember – very few people succeed in business without a degree of confidence. I have worked with many leaders over the years who were limited by their lack of confidence. They were really good at the 'doing' elements of their job but this basic competence was no longer enough – not when they needed to exercise leadership in a way that had real impact and could influence real results.

Confidence isn't just something you work towards, attain and then forget about – it's something you have to work on at all times, no matter what stage of your career, and no matter what level, job or industry you're working in.

Without confidence, you can do little; with it, you can do anything!

Of course, confidence can wax and wane throughout our lives. It's boosted when we accomplish something great or when we get good feedback from those we trust, but it can take a hit when we fall short of the mark, or we're criticised, rejected or simply feel a lack of external recognition. We're only human after all. Moving away from being reliant on external affirmation to prop up our self-worth is, therefore, vital. We must take ownership for the actions needed to sustain our confidence.

Often people think of confidence as something that the lucky few are born with and the rest are left wishing for. This is not true. Confidence is not a personality trait or a fixed attribute; it's the outcome of the thoughts we think and the actions we take. Confidence is learnable.

Confidence isn't based on our actual ability to succeed at a task but on our *belief* in our ability to succeed. It is the expectation of a positive outcome – regardless of whether this relates to our belief in our ability to speak in front of a large audience, to learn new technology, to lead a team, to handle confrontation, to change jobs and careers, or to start a business.

With consistent effort, and the courage to take a risk, we can gradually expand our confidence and, with it, our capacity to build more of it. That's what this book will help you do.

How this book is organised

Developing confidence has many aspects, and you may find you're stronger in some aspects of your confidence than in others. I've had clients say to me the process is like peeling back an onion – and to really develop your confidence from the inside out, you need to peel that onion.

In this book, I show you how to peel back the layers and work on four key aspects of confidence. First, I provide important linkages to why confidence is critical to leadership success at both the individual and team level. Then I dive into specifics, providing practical ways to build confidence in an authentic way for sustainable success in the four key areas. I show you how to:

1. *Show up* as the real you and the best version of you as a leader

2. *Stand up* for yourself, your team, your values and your point of view

3. *Speak up* and have a voice and be able to influence

4. *Step up* your performance, your impact and, ultimately, how you exercise leadership.

Simply *feeling* confident isn't enough. You have to do the work. But with an expectation of success, you can try new things – form new partnerships, contribute to shared success, and revel in small wins that move you toward bigger goals.

Lots of books are available on confidence, but this one shows you how confidence is critical to your leadership and how you can use it to increase your value to yourself, your team and your organisation. Ultimately, real confidence is the key ingredient that will help you to maximise your leadership potential.

How to use this book

The best books (in my opinion) are the ones that inspire you, educate you, push you, challenge you to think differently and, above all else, give you practical strategies that you can implement in your life straightaway. So it would be foolish of me to write a book on confidence where I didn't do all of those things. Throughout this book, you'll find practical tips and strategies to build and sustain your leadership confidence.

You'll also read real-life case studies and stories from colleagues and people I have worked with, and from my own personal journey developing confidence. These allow you to see the strategies in action, and also see you're not alone.

At the end of each chapter, you'll be asked to 'Check your confidence' through a series of questions that relate to the content you've just read. Read them and go away and think about them. Jot answers and thoughts down in a notebook that you can refer to over time and track how your confidence has improved.

In the last chapter of this book, you have the chance to assess your confidence using a self-assessment tool I developed based on my work. Use this to help you determine which of the four confidence stages (show up, stand up, speak up and step up) you need to work on first. You can then continue to use this tool to help you at different points in your confidence journey. This is how you truly learn to not only build confidence but also sustain it.

It's your job to set direction and determine outcomes, and that only happens when you feel confident in yourself. Sound good? I thought so. Let's begin.

PART I
LEARN

SHOW UP

STAND UP

SPEAK UP

STEP UP

Do you ever wonder what it is about some people that makes them so confident? We know confidence when we see it, don't we? Or we think we do. Confident people seem completely comfortable in their own skin, to know who they are, and to believe in themselves and their ability to be successful. They take action and don't seem to let anything hold them back.

No single definition exists for what confidence is, yet it is so important in our lives – and, more specifically, so important in our leadership.

Like confidence, no one-size-fits-all definition exists for leadership. And for that I am grateful! Imagine if we were all trying to lead with the same style, characteristics and traits. We would all be pretty boring and uninspiring (the opposite of what being a leader is). We do, however, have a fairly commonly accepted set of competencies and capabilities that are important for leadership – things like influence, accountability, strategic thinking, integrity, vision, decision-making and relationship management. Yet, doing any one of these things takes confidence.

Whichever way you look at it, confidence is a critical foundation for leadership. In fact, you could say it is the ultimate leadership skill.

The ability to lead with confidence, therefore, is not a 'nice to have'; it is a 'must have'. Confidence separates average leaders from great leaders and, without it, you will never maximise your own leadership potential.

In this part of the book, I help you understand why confidence plays such an important role in your leadership potential.

CHAPTER 1
MAXIMISE YOUR LEADERSHIP POTENTIAL

As far as the American public was concerned, the 1970 Apollo 13 mission was just another routine space flight. That was until we heard the words, 'Houston, we have a problem' (well, in the movie anyway).

I love the true story the movie was based on, which revolves around NASA Flight Director Gene Kranz (portrayed by Ed Harris). Here was a leader who wouldn't submit to defeat – even when it was staring him in the face – and who wouldn't let his team accept defeat either.

Kranz expertly marshalled his resources with his instruction to 'work the problem', enabling everyone to play their role in resolving the crisis. For every seemingly impossible situation, his response was simple – find a way to make it work.

Of course, the movie highlighted just how infectious his confidence was! 'We've never lost an American in space and we sure as hell ain't gonna lose one on my watch,' he tells his assembled flight team. 'Failure is not an option!'

Would this have been so inspiring (and effective) if Kranz wasn't able to lead with confidence? If he wasn't able to inspire his team to believe that they could make the impossible happen?

Saving the Apollo 13 mission took a massive team effort – from the grounded pilot brought into the simulator to find a successful re-entry approach, to the NASA staff given a box of everything in the shuttle and instructed to use it to make a 'square peg fit a round hole'.

In today's ever-changing business landscape, we desperately need leaders like Gene Kranz – leaders who can ... well ... lead, and who lead with confidence. Because exercising leadership like this is so much more than having the competence to get the job done. You must have the confidence to make an impact beyond your wildest dreams.

Competence versus confidence

Francisco Dao is a speaker on organisational performance and strategy, and he sees self-confidence as the fundamental basis from which leadership grows. As he puts it in his 'Without confidence, there is no leadership' *Inc.* article, 'Trying to teach leadership without first building confidence is like building a house on a foundation of sand. It may have a nice coat of paint, but it is ultimately shaky at best.'

A strong foundation of confidence is needed because leadership is seldom easy. Decisions must be made under time pressure and with many shades of grey. You have to inspire your team through a world of complexity and uncertainty, unite them, and give them drive and great purpose. Without confidence, how long do you think you will last? This is especially the case in today's disruptive climate.

Over the course of my career, I have worked with some outstanding leaders. (And some leaders who were not so outstanding, I have to say!) Despite vast differences in styles and personalities, the ones I would say were great leaders were able to strike an important balance between competence and confidence.

Confidence separates average leaders from great leaders. If you're competent in your job, you can tick all the boxes and get the job done. You have the ability required for your role, the right level of skills, the right level of knowledge and the right capacity. However, being competent in your job is no longer enough if you are striving to be a great leader. You must be able to cultivate a culture of confidence in your team and everyone around you so they too believe they can do whatever it is you want them to do. That means you must first have confidence in yourself and your leadership ability. You need to lead with confidence, and so have the ability to inspire confidence in everyone else around you, so they too can achieve great feats.

Cultivating confidence

Cultivating confidence with others starts from the minute we walk into a room, the minute we open our mouths and speak. Often those judgments are made in less than a minute and within seconds. (In fact, a series of experiments by Princeton psychologists Janine Willis and Alexander Todorov revealed forming a first impression of a stranger takes a mere tenth of a second.)

If, based on how they show up, we believe a leader to be confident, we will assume that they are competent. If we get any sense of a lack of confidence, however, we will assume a lack of competence. This may not be fair, but that's what judgment is all about!

These judgments also have to do with people's assumptions about what a leader should look like. If you show up and seem anxious and insecure, or seem to have some self-doubt, you won't be perceived as a leader because people will think you are a liability, regardless of your actual level of competence and skill to do the job.

So, in order to cultivate confidence in other people, you must first believe and have confidence in your own ability to weather the storms, to perform well under pressure, to learn from mistakes and bounce back, to create and innovate, and to keep raising the bar and driving higher levels of performance. Setting direction, executing strategy and creating an engaging environment for employees to bring their best all takes confidence. You must have confidence and belief in your own ability before you can instil these in others.

I'm not talking about arrogance here – and there's a big difference between that and confidence. I love how psychologist and body language expert Amy Cuddy describes this difference, explaining confidence is a tool and arrogance is a weapon. Arrogance, or overconfidence, has caused the downfall of many a leader and I'm sure you can think of some pretty public figures, and perhaps some not so public, where this has occurred. Overconfident leaders lack the capacity to question themselves, have little humility or vulnerability and often engage in too much risk taking – all things you want to avoid.

When I talk about real *confidence*, I'm talking about an authentic confidence that is built from the inside out – not bravado and not overconfidence. I'm talking about having the ability to be confident and to build confidence in others but to be humble and vulnerable at the same time.

Taking your leadership potential to the max

Over 100 years ago, William James, a psychologist teaching at Harvard University, wrote that the reason so many people never fulfil their potential is not because of a lack of intelligence, opportunity or resources, but because of a lack of belief, or faith, in themselves. I think this is so true.

Nothing is better than feeling confident, and having the courage to face challenges, place yourself in the path of opportunities and take risks head on. Often confidence gives you the ability to first put your hand up for that more senior leadership role and then be successful at nailing the selection process. Without it, you may have all the competence and skills required to do the job but just never feel ready to go for it. Having confidence like this enables you to realise your potential.

Without confidence, you can give up too easily, refuse to believe an opportunity is possible and, therefore, make limiting decisions about how you lead, what you lead and whether even to lead.

Confidence helps us maximise our leadership potential.

Just think of someone who you say is confident. Chances are they're poised, hopeful and positive. They know their strengths and weaknesses. It is this that makes all the difference to the performance of your organisation.

In research work, professor of business at Harvard Business School, Rosabeth Moss Kanter, compared companies and sporting teams that had long winning streaks and long losing streaks. In the *Harvard Business Review* article 'Cultivate a culture of confidence', where she discussed some of her findings, she argued 'self-confidence, combined with confidence in one another and in the organization, motivates winners to make the extra push that can provide the margin of victory.' She explained that the lesson for leaders is to build the cornerstones of confidence and maintain a culture of confidence. Doing so will ensure that, when you are faced with the inevitable downturns in performance, you are much better placed to lead through them.

Learn to SCALE

To capture the link between confidence and your leadership potential, I developed the SCALE Leadership Confidence Model, shown in figure 1.1. This shows how you can move from building competence and capability in yourself, to inspiring confidence in others, and highlights how that relates to how you are maximising your own leadership potential. The following sections take you through each of the stages in more detail.

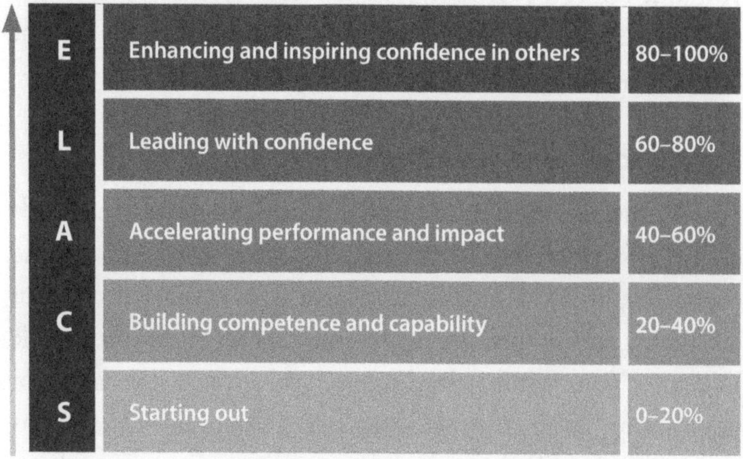

E	Enhancing and inspiring confidence in others	80–100%
L	Leading with confidence	60–80%
A	Accelerating performance and impact	40–60%
C	Building competence and capability	20–40%
S	Starting out	0–20%

Figure 1.1: The SCALE Leadership Confidence Model

Starting out

The first level of the model shows the first 0 to 20 per cent range of your leadership potential. Being at this level usually means you don't have a huge amount of confidence. You might be here because you've just been appointed to your first leadership role, or you've been promoted into a more senior leadership role or even a role of greater influence. You may have taken on additional tasks because your boss or someone else encouraged you, saying you'd 'be good at it', even though you might not agree. And some people around you might be questioning if you have 'what it takes' to do the job.

When you are starting out, you are at the very beginning of working towards your leadership potential. We are all starting out at new things all the time in life, but the more you take on new roles and responsibilities, and try new ways of being and operating, the quicker you will move up the model towards gaining greater confidence.

Building competence and capability

As you move into the 20 to 40 per cent range of your leadership potential, you begin to build your competence and capability, and the impact you have is often based on your ability to complete the technical elements of the work. Whether your work is leading a team, speaking on stage or negotiating large contracts, you generally build the competency-based skills first.

Building these skills is important, and you need to have the competencies that are required for the work. Leadership competencies are observable and measurable skills and behaviours that contribute to your overall leadership and career success. Yet they alone are not enough. You must also have confidence and belief in your own ability to be able to make a bigger impact.

Thankfully, as you build these competencies, your confidence will start to grow. As you perform well in the 'doing' elements of your role, you get good feedback and start to build your belief about yourself. You then start to see your success in the role is possible.

Accelerating performance and impact

As you build both your competence and confidence, you begin to accelerate your performance and impact, moving into 40 to 60 per cent of your leadership potential.

In this stage, you're taking more risks, moving outside your comfort zone and putting your hand up to get involved beyond your scope. You're feeling much more comfortable and confident in what you are doing and how you are leading. The confidence you are building allows your competence to shine, provides you with influence and power in the right forums and means you can stop questioning your ability.

This has a flow-on effect to the impact you make to those around you, and starts to accelerate your performance.

Leading with confidence

When you start leading with confidence, you have a core belief in your ability to be successful. Once you reach this stage, you are at 60 to 80 per cent of your leadership potential.

You understand that confidence is a critical leadership skill and important to maintain. You have a strong understanding of what it takes to show up as the best version of you and how this really supports you. Your confidence also has a 'realness' to it, and you have an influential voice and a strong leadership presence. You also role-model this confidence to those around you and are respected for it.

You know how to celebrate your achievements in a humble manner, and accept your strengths and weaknesses in a balanced way. You listen to what others have to say and surround yourself with colleagues who will challenge and support you.

Enhancing and inspiring confidence in others

Reaching the golden 80 to 100 per cent of your leadership potential comes when you extend your confidence to those around you, and start to inspire confidence in them. Without this extension to others, real leadership has not been achieved!

Leading with confidence is the essential ingredient in enhancing and inspiring confidence in others. Confidence breeds confidence, after all.

When you are at this point in the SCALE Leadership Confidence Model, you're maximising your own leadership potential along with the leadership potential in your teams. That means you are actively building a culture of confidence and maximising the performance of your whole business and entire organisation. Isn't this a great place to be?

It's only when you start leading with confidence and inspiring confidence in others that you are truly exercising great leadership.

Where are you now?

Consider where you are right now on the SCALE Leadership Confidence Model – and, more importantly, where do you want to be?

Stop and reflect

As you head into the remainder of this book, start to think about where you might be sitting on your own leadership journey. Are you just starting to build your competence and not yet feeling confident about your ability to succeed?
Or are you sitting midway on the SCALE and feel like you've hit a bit of a brick wall? Are you now looking to step up and accelerate your leadership potential?

Remember – while the principles of confidence in leadership may seem relatively simple, the building and sustaining of confidence requires real work. So even when you make it to the top of the model, you need to be able to continuously work at sustaining your confidence. You will at times find you are back to square one and back to working on the basics, especially if you leave your job, start something new or step up to exercise leadership differently (see chapter 5 for more on this).

As journalists Katty Kay and Claire Shipman wrote in *The Confidence Code*, 'Confidence is hard to define but easy to recognize. With it, you can take on the world; without it, you live stuck at the starting block of your potential.'

Chase your fear

The following comes from my interview with Kate Hughes, former Chief Risk Officer at Telstra.

When I first took on the Chief Risk Officer role, I'd never been a CRO before, and I was managing risks I was completely unfamiliar with. I didn't have a lot of market and credit risk experience and was acutely aware of how important it was to be good at this. I think you know when you don't have that confidence, and people can smell the doubt and insecurity on you.

Every night I would come home and lie on the couch and fear that I was not doing this right; that I was going to miss something really important and that I wasn't capable of doing this job. It was that total fraud moment, that imposter syndrome that we have so often. [See chapter 5 for more on the imposter syndrome.]

My husband said to me, 'Kate, there's a bit of a pattern here with you, do you know what it is?' And I said, 'I keep taking jobs that I'm not capable of doing?' He said, 'No, you keep taking jobs that you're really frightened of. So, do you think maybe that's because you want to conquer them? You're chasing it down. You're looking for it. Isn't that the very reason you get out of bed every day? Isn't that why you do it? Because you're taking on the unknown and you want to win at it. You want to build that confidence. You want to build that expertise.'

He was right. I desperately wanted to be confident in it. I knew I needed to reach for those moments that would probably strike fear in my heart because I didn't know how to do everything. Those things were motivating me the most. It was a deliberate confidence building exercise.

I remember when I first got to Telstra, I thought, *What do I know here? I know big corporations. I know risk management really well. I know compliance. I know retail businesses.* And I was ticking off all the things I was confident at and then stopping and thinking about what I didn't know.

I thought, *I don't really know how the network works. I didn't really know how all of the technical stuff works, which is the key to the decisions we have to make.* I remember sitting down and asking the Head of Networks at the time to take me through everything from the day telephones first existed to today. It took him five hours to go through it but I remember walking out thinking, *Good! One more. Got that one. Know it. Confident.*

So recognise what you don't know and then actively chase it down.

Check your confidence

1. How would you rate your current level of competence as a leader?

2. How confident are you feeling about how you are exercising leadership right now?

3. Where do you currently see yourself on the SCALE Leadership Confidence Model?

4. Where would you like to be?

Now you have a better understanding of why it's important to increase your confidence, not just your competence, in order to truly maximise your leadership potential, it's time to get started on the nitty-gritty and look at how you do that. This is the focus of part II, where we explore the Real Confidence Model.

PART II

LEAD

STAND UP SPEAK UP STEP UP SHOW UP

In part I, we discussed why it's important to develop your confidence as a leader. Now the real question is: How? How do you build your confidence in all areas of your leadership?

You will need to develop the four areas in my Real Confidence Model, shown in the following figure.

The Real Confidence Model

As shown in the figure, the four main areas to develop are:

1. **Show up:** How do you confidently show up as the best version of yourself? The three key skills we focus on here are self-awareness, authenticity and strength.

2. **Stand up:** How do you stand up with confidence for what you believe in, and against what you don't support? We look at your values and purpose, and how resilient you are.

3. **Speak up:** How do you speak up confidently and influence? Here we assess your voice, your leadership presence and your impact as a leader.

4. **Step up:** How do you step up your leadership so you're performing at your peak? Our focus here is on developing your mindset, brand and sponsorships.

The chapters in part II dive deep into each of these four areas – so let's get started.

CHAPTER 2
SHOW UP

Have you ever been in a relationship with someone – whether it is your partner, friend or colleague – where you feel the other person just gets you? They know and appreciate the essence of who you are. You know that they trust you and because of these factors, in turn, you trust them too. You love being around them for the very fact that you can be who you really are and they accept you.

How good is that feeling? How *confident* does that make you feel? How *confident* does this make your leadership?

In leadership, having the ability to *show up* with *real* confidence means you know yourself, you can be yourself and you show up as the best version of yourself.

This is more than getting out of bed, splashing some water on your face and fronting up at your desk hoping you can cope with what the day throws at you.

When I talk about *showing up* with confidence as a leader, I'm talking about doing the work required so you can think, feel and act with confidence in yourself, your ability, your impact and your value. You believe you can draw on what you are great at and exercise leadership well. You believe what you're good at is important, and that it's aligned with how you are working and leading. You believe that you are valuable and valued.

> *When you show up with confidence, you are better able to connect with your team and increase your leadership influence.*

Building confidence from the inside out

Showing up as truly confident over a sustained period of time is something that needs to be built from the inside out. This is real work that takes a good level of consciousness. You can't just stumble upon this kind of confidence. Knowing yourself, being yourself and showing up as the best version of yourself doesn't just suddenly happen.

Likewise, 'faking it until you make it' only gets you so far and for so long. Trying to pretend you have the confidence needed to get the job done can be exhausting. Sure, it can work for some people at some points in time, but faking it on an ongoing basis and not doing the work to really build your confidence is not sustainable for great leadership.

True confidence is also not about imitating someone else, or someone else's leadership style. I have worked with many leaders over the years who have tried to be tough, tried to be hard, and tried to imitate someone else's leadership style and approach. They thought if that style worked for the other person, surely it would work for them.

While having role models and learning from the experience of other successful leaders is important, you cannot be successful by trying to be them.

As successful American businessman, Kevin W. Sharer, who was Jack Welch's assistant in the 1980s, was quoted as saying in the *Harvard Business Review* article 'Discovering your authentic leadership', 'Everyone wanted to be like Jack … Leadership has many voices. You need to be who you are, not try to emulate somebody else.'

Be yourself

Sean, a client of mine (name changed), had worked in specialist roles for most of his career until he was appointed to run a large, high-profile business. It was his first role at this level and with this degree of exposure in the organisation.

A lot of pressure was also being applied in this part of the business because it wasn't performing well. So, Sean went in and started leading like his boss, who was very 'in your face' and driven and who used the old command-and-control style. This was totally against his own leadership style and what had made him successful to this point in his career, but he felt this was what it took to lead in this organisation.

After six months, the pressure was mounting, performance still hadn't improved and Sean was deeply unhappy. He didn't change his leadership approach, however, and just kept driving his people even harder. Trust and empowerment was low and micro-management high. Eventually he was asked to leave.

When he reflected with me on his leadership during this time, he realised that he had taken on what he thought he should do because his boss led this way. He hadn't led in his own leadership style, and this had caused a real impact to his confidence.

Sean worked on his values and his leadership purpose and became really clear on how he needed to be authentic from this point on. Since then, he has been appointed into a new senior role in another organisation. He is leading with authenticity. He has a team that is high-performing, empowered and trusted. He is being himself. He has once again found his confidence and this is having a very positive impact on his performance and the performance of his teams and business.

Learn to show up

How do we start this work so we can show up with confidence? It comes down to being aware, being real and being strong. In other words, showing up requires three key skills:

1. Self-awareness (be aware)
2. Authenticity (be real)
3. Strength (be strong).

These three skills are highlighted in figure 2.1, and discussed further in the following sections.

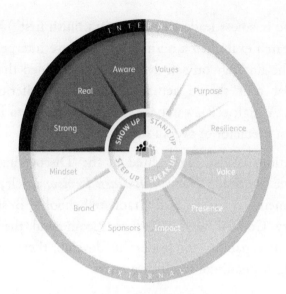

Figure 2.1: Show up

Self-awareness – be aware

In his book *Primal Leadership*, psychologist and author Daniel Goleman identifies that 'the first task in management has nothing to do with leading others; step one poses that challenge of knowing and managing oneself.'

Having a strong sense of self-awareness is now seen as a critical trait for successful leaders, and is increasingly being reported in studies as the one quality that trumps all.

One particularly enlightening study conducted in 2010 by Green Peak Partners and Cornell's School of Industrial and Labor Relations examined 72 executives at public and private companies with revenues from $50 million to $5 billion. (Their findings were published in the article, 'When it comes to business leadership, nice guys finish first'.) While the research examined a number of executive interpersonal traits, the findings on self-awareness determined that this particular trait should actually be the top criterion for success. A high self-awareness score was shown to be the strongest predictor of overall success.

In addition, as also highlighted in the 'Discovering your authentic leadership' *Harvard Business Review* article, when the 75 members of Stanford Graduate School of Business's Advisory Council were asked to recommend the most important capability for leaders to develop, their answers were nearly unanimous: self-awareness.

Without self-awareness we cannot understand our strengths and weaknesses. We cannot understand ourselves sufficiently to know what it means to be authentic in our leadership. We are not aware of what motivates us, what drives our decision-making, and what people we need around us to build the best teams. Self-awareness exercises are critical to building a sense of self and the confidence to show up as a strong and influential leader.

When you think about yourself, your strengths and your weaknesses, you need to reflect both inside-out and outside-in. In 'What self-awareness really is (and how to cultivate it)', a *Harvard Business Review* article from 2018, Dr Tasha Eurich distinguishes between our internal self-awareness, which is *how well you know yourself,* and our external self-awareness, which is *how well you understand how others see you.*

To become truly aware you need to have a high internal self-awareness *and* a high external self-awareness. But what does this mean and how do you achieve it? One simple framework to help you extend your self-awareness to both internal and external awareness focuses on the three YOUs, as shown in figure 2.2.

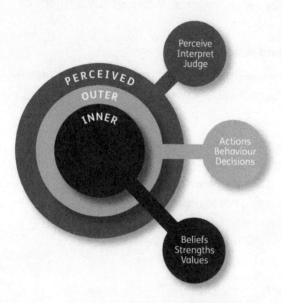

Figure 2.2: The three YOUs

The three YOUs can be understood as follows:

1. **Inner you:** What your beliefs, strengths and values are. What drives you? What is core to you?

2. **Outer you:** How you express or use your beliefs, strengths and values via your actions, behaviours and decisions. How do your beliefs and values contribute to

the decisions you make? What impact does this have on your behaviours and your actions?

3. **Perceived you:** How others interpret your behaviour. Do your actions match others' perceptions of you?

When we have a strong self-awareness of our real selves in these three areas, we are able to be truly authentic.

Stop and reflect

Spend some time now reflecting on each of the three YOUs by considering these questions.

Inner you:

- ► What am I trying to achieve?
- ► What am I great at?
- ► What gives me energy?
- ► What am I not so great at?
- ► What needs to change?
- ► What do I really value?
- ► What do I truly believe in?

Outer you:

- ► What decisions am I making?
- ► Are my decisions congruent with what I believe in?
- ► Am I behaving in line with my values?
- ► How consistent is my behaviour?

Perceived you:

- ► What impact am I having on those around me?
- ► What feedback have I received?
- ► What do you notice from your responses to these questions? Which areas could you improve?

Authenticity – be real

People want to be led by people they trust. This trust is earned when you demonstrate authenticity – that is, when you show the real you. That means you do what you say you will, your actions are aligned with your values and your motives are easily identified by those around you.

This is why admired leaders are often described as 'grounded'. They have no secret agenda. These people are likeable and, more importantly for leadership, they are trusted and respected. They are humble.

I bet you can think of people like this in your life straightaway – the ones whose impression has never left you because they embodied all of these attributes. Perhaps they even inspired you to be a better version of you.

Without confidence in showing up, our ability to convey authenticity, earn trust, build connections and have sponsors fly our flag is greatly diminished. When we are our true selves, we are happier, more energetic, more productive and more confident. An ease comes with knowing ourselves well enough to have the courage to be authentic in all areas of our life – and this also means having the courage to be vulnerable.

In an interview with Martha Rosenberg, vulnerability expert Brené Brown said, 'Vulnerability is the birthplace of connection and the path to the feeling of worthiness. If it doesn't feel vulnerable, the sharing is probably not constructive.'

So, just being real and authentic isn't enough. To take this authenticity from the inside to the outside, you need to build the courage to be vulnerable. Vulnerability creates real connections and builds trust and this is what great leadership is all about. Having the courage to be vulnerable, to reveal who you really are and what has made you this way is at the centre of authenticity.

Maren Kate Donovan was the CEO of Zirtual, a company that in the words of *Fortune* magazine 'imploded overnight', basically through not controlling its cash flow. Donovan shares a lesson about vulnerability learned from this experience in her blog, *Escaping the 9 to 5*. She begins by recalling a poignant dinner conversation in which a guest said, 'I just don't know how you could have made those mistakes.'

Donovan says, 'In Silicon Valley, admitting mistakes and showing your vulnerable side is one of the biggest social faux pas that I'm tired of trying to follow'. Instead she chose 'brutal vulnerability' – to be authentic, to seek help and ultimately inspire people.

Brett Clark is another CEO who includes authenticity and humility in his definition of good leadership. In Kirsten Galliott's 2017 'View from the Top' article in the Qantas *Inflight* magazine he was quoted as saying, 'Authenticity is a word that gets thrown around a lot but I really do believe in it. I've got to be who I am; I can't present another version of me. People see through that straightaway.' When asked what happens on the days that you're not feeling confident, his answer is, 'You say so. I don't think you can pretend. We all have good days and days that we hoped would be better.'

Vulnerability is the foundation for all other attributes of authenticity, because it determines whether or not others can genuinely relate to you. No-one else is like you in the world. If you are successful at expressing your uniqueness, others are more likely to perceive you as authentic. And if you need a simple way to frame this, remember the quote commonly attributed to Oscar Wilde: 'Be yourself; everyone else is already taken.'

Get real

The following comes from my interview with Kate Hughes, former Chief Risk Officer at Telstra.

I always had parents who were very clear with me about speaking the truth and allowing myself to be vulnerable. I was not ashamed at all of showing emotion, of bringing my real self to a situation, and I think that became apparent when I joined the corporate environment.

I went straight out of university into a graduate role and people were always astounded at how honest I could be and I thought, *Isn't everyone like that?* It was only when I stood back and watched that I noticed the leaders in the organisation were role-modelling this very stoic, 'don't show your emotions, don't be vulnerable' thing.

I remember looking at that and thinking, *Is that how I have to be now?* I found that really hard after being raised a certain way and having had success with being authentic.

What I actually then found was that when I was more authentic in the face of everyone else not being, that resonated with a lot of people.

Strength – be strong

What are you great at? Who are you at your best? What really energises you?

Exploiting and building on what we've already got makes sense. Understanding and using our strengths is about focusing on the things we are great at and which give us the most energy. Positive psychology tells us we get much more bang for our buck if we focus on our strengths rather than trying to boost our weaknesses. This doesn't mean ignoring our weaknesses, but is about deciding what we put most emphasis on.

As far back as 1967, management guru Peter Drucker wrote the following in his book *The Effective Executive:*

> The effective executive makes strengths productive.
> To achieve results, one has to use all available strengths
> … These strengths are the true opportunities. To
> make strength productive is the unique purpose of the
> organisation … It cannot overcome the weaknesses with
> which each of us is endowed, but it can make them
> irrelevant.

▌▌ Stop and reflect

When it comes to leadership, the underlying element of self-confidence is an understanding of what you have accomplished and what you feel you can do next.

Consider what has enabled you to accomplish your achievements to date. When it comes to finding these sources, you want to focus on the positives and your moments of triumph; think about those opportunities where you shone, helping yourself and your team achieve a goal.

Ask yourself:

- ► What do I do well?
- ► What am I often recognised for?
- ► What do I find energising?

Any number of self-reflection tools can help facilitate a deeper understanding of your strengths, and help you develop a deeper understanding of how you operate and who you are at your best. One example is the Strengths Profiler, which is a workplace tool developed by Alex Linley and his UK-based team that draws on the latest positive psychology research. I use this with leaders to help them pinpoint and leverage their strengths, as well as recognising areas of weakness. The Strengths Profiler helps us focus on four key areas:

1. **Realised strengths** – you perform well in these areas, they give you energy and you use these strengths often.

2. **Unrealised strengths** – you perform well using these strengths and they give you energy but you don't use them as often.

3. **Learned behaviours** – while you perform well in these areas, they de-energise you.

4. **Weaknesses** – you don't perform well in these traits or areas, and they de-energise you.

You can use these areas to draw four columns or a grid on some paper. Then consider the following:

► What are my core strengths?

► How often do I use them?

► How energised do I feel when using them?

Use your answers to these questions to complete your columns or grid. This then enables you to develop a much deeper understanding of your strengths and to create strategies to optimise your performance and potential.

From a leadership perspective, when people use their strengths they perform better, achieve results faster and feel more engaged and energised. Strengths also help encourage engagement with those you lead. So when you extend your focus from your own strengths to those of your team, you begin to have real impact. When you have a team focused on optimising their strengths, you have a team more motivated and more engaged – and more confident! Who wouldn't want that?

Eat from the energy menu

Being strong is also about having strong physical and mental wellbeing. For example, I know I will be in a really good place, and feel stronger and more confident, when I exercise regularly and can fit in some meditation at some points through the week (even if this is just in the cracks of my day).

Many of the leaders I work with now, however, are extremely time poor, with most working anywhere up to 16 hours a day. So, what gives? Our energy and eventually our health and our home life, that's what – the very things we live for.

How can we develop a real understanding of ourselves when we are running so hard just to get stuff done? As already discussed, this self-awareness and strength is at the core of being able to show up as the best version of ourselves.

When we feel depleted of energy and when we're not doing the things we love to do outside of work, our confidence and our ability to show up at work starts to deteriorate. We struggle to make decisions at work and lose the ability, desire or need to connect with our team members.

Most often, we think of this as a time-management problem – that is, we don't have enough of it or we aren't managing it correctly. However, time is a finite resource; we can never get more of it. We will always face an increasing pressure on our performance, so approaching the problem as a time-management issue just makes us feel worse. We actually need to look at this from the perspective of our energy levels.

The good news is that your energy can be restored and renewed, and doing so is a much better option to help you meet the challenges of everyday work, while allowing you to show up as the best version of yourself. If ever there was a time to manage your energy and wellbeing so that your leadership is sustainable, it is now.

So how do you top up your energy levels to stay on top of your performance and ability to *show up* with confidence at work?

While you might immediately picture crossed-legged, lotus-positioned figures practising meditation, this is only one strategy that some of us employ (and only one style of meditation). The activities that energise one person may not energise another. You need to find what works for you.

Stop and reflect

To start uncovering what activities energise you, take note of your energy levels at particular times of the day. When do you feel particularly energised? When do you want to slump and just watch Netflix? Try jotting your thoughts down in a journal or notebook for a week, and see what patterns emerge. Are you a morning person or an afternoon person?

What activities do you do on a weekly basis to help you rest and recover? Do you walk the dog every morning? Or do you prefer a personal training session, yoga or just sitting down and reading? Recording these activities will help you come up with your own 'energy menu', and mean you can 'place an order' from these activities whenever you're feeling drained.

These *intentional activities* deserve a permanent place in our diaries if we are committed to being the best version of ourselves. They may be physical or mental, or involve a change of environment or connection with others.

I've started doing this myself and have found my 'energy menu' is most useful if I have a range of activities to draw upon in four key areas:

1. Brain
2. Body

3. Relationships

4. Environment.

To help get you thinking on what activities might work for you, here are some of mine from across the four key areas that I book into my diary well in advance:

► morning exercise;

► time at the park with Molly, my gorgeous cavoodle;

► mindfulness practice (I'm still in the experimental phase with this one);

► dinners with friends and family;

► holidays and long weekends; and

► reading a great book (like this one, of course).

When something is affecting your self-confidence, you are more equipped to deal with it if you have things to look forward to during the day or, even better, have taken time early each morning to reset and enhance your mindset. Doing so means the day is no longer about what is affecting us and, instead, is reframed to reflect a balance of everything that matters to and energises us.

Be mindful of not only the *number* of activities in your calendar, but also the *type* of activities, and whether they enhance or deplete your energy and confidence. If certain activities are depleting your energy, could you reshuffle their order, or outsource or automate them – or even balance them out by adding activities that enhance your wellbeing?

While to-do lists may keep growing, your ability to manage these is determined by your commitment to your 'to-be' list. So I invite you all to challenge your jam-packed calendars and find some time for you – even if it's only in the 'cracks' of your day.

A great and confident leader is a person who is committed to being the best human they can possibly be.

What's in your 'Happiness Pie'?

Life is like a big pie with lots of different flavours. Yours might comprise work, community, family, friends and exercise. The sections of your pie you devote the most energy to determine your happiness levels, and contribute to not only your sense of fulfilment, but also your confidence and ability to show up in life.

Author and professor in psychology at the University of California, Sonja Lyubomirsky, developed these concepts into what she calls the 'Happiness Pie'. Lyubomirsky argues that 50 per cent of the differences in people's happiness levels can be attributed to genetic set points, while 10 per cent is determined by circumstances and 40 per cent by the choices we make every day.

You could easily assume that the genetic chunk – accounting for 50 per cent – is the main determinant of our happiness levels. That is, the make-up of our genes could be enough to limit our ability to achieve happiness. However, this is not the case. In fact, our choices about what we do and think in the 40 per cent portion of the pie could potentially prevent disadvantageous genes from expressing themselves.

Lyubomirsky's research is empowering because it means that we potentially have far more control over our happiness than we may have thought. Being born with great genes or within the right set of circumstances does not necessarily lead to a path of success or happiness. In fact, you could say many leaders have had the odds set against them in terms of circumstances or genetics, and yet have still managed to create a happy and meaningful life for themselves.

Much research has explored how happy people think and act differently from those who are less happy. This research shows happier people tend to:

- pursue goals;
- practise gratitude;
- nurture their relationships;
- have self-compassion; and
- focus on their strengths.

What behaviours or thoughts do you have and to what extent do they serve you? What new ones could you adopt? What could you let go?

Just as you might be fussy about what goes in the pies you eat, be equally fussy about what you put in your Happiness Pie.

 Check your confidence

1. How would you rate your level of self-awareness on a scale of 1 to 10? (Rate yourself between 10 for extremely self-aware and 1 for not very self-aware.)

2. Reflect on the three YOUs in the 'Stop and reflect' exercise earlier in this chapter. What do you notice? Which areas need the most improvement?

3. Think of three leaders you would describe as authentic. What do you respect in each of them? What do they do well? How could you apply some of these strategies to become more authentic yourself?

4. What are your strengths and how well do you use them? You may like to try the Strengths Profiler to help you with this. (Go to strengthsprofile.com for more information.)

5. When are you at your best? To discover this, try jotting down your energy levels during the course of each day over a period of a week. What activities help you rest and relax?

6. Start mapping your own 'energy menu' that includes a range of activities across the four key areas: brain, body, relationships and environment.

How did you do? These check points shouldn't be rushed, so spend some more time with each point and question if you need. Once you know what it takes to show up as the best version of you, you're ready to move on to the next stage of the Confidence Model – standing up.

CHAPTER 3
STAND UP

Think for a moment about Richard Branson talking about gender equality, or any of the following expounding on the issues they are passionate about:

► Rosie Batty on domestic violence;
► Eddie Mabo on land rights;
► Sheryl Sandberg on leaning in;
► Nelson Mandela on freedom and equality;
► David Morrison on gender quality in the Australian Army;
► Alan Joyce on same-sex marriage;
► Al Gore on climate change; and
► Fred Hollows on preventable loss of sight.

No matter the politics, religion or business, these leaders, and many more like them, have one thing in common. They *stand up* with confidence for what they believe in and inspire us all.

Leadership takes many forms and there is no one-size-fits-all approach (luckily!). But in all my years working in, on and around leadership, the thing that I see as mattering the most is the ability to stand up for what you believe in. As a leader, you need to speak up when no-one else will and lead change. You need to be visible, make unpopular decisions and go slow in order to go fast. You must stand alone in a crowd and have the confidence to believe in yourself.

You don't need to be standing up for worldwide rights and you don't need to be the Dalai Lama, but you do need to stand up for what you deem right, fair and important.

Let me give you an example of standing up from my own experience. I once worked with a leader who was tested with a serious issue that affected his customers, stakeholders and entire organisation. It soon became a very public issue. From the very outset, he took the lead and remained calm and rational, demonstrating his ability to take charge under pressure. He could have easily entered the 'blame game' by finding fault with individuals or previous decisions, but he didn't.

When he came under pressure to make quick decisions, he took a stand on a more considered approach that would ensure a much more sustainable outcome. He stood up and took personal responsibility. He said if anyone had to take 'the fall', it would be him. He encouraged full disclosure and led the development of an effective plan for recovery. He showed empathy for those involved. Ultimately, he was able to stand up with confidence and lead through these issues even though it would have felt at times like he was standing alone.

Stop and reflect

Think about the last time you stood up for what you believed in. When have you stood up with your team to support them to achieve something that felt out of reach? When did you last voice an opinion that was against that of the majority?

In today's world, we need leaders who are not afraid to stand up for themselves, as well as their people.

For, with or against?

Organisations and society in general are becoming increasingly impatient with leaders who don't do what they say they will do and don't take a stand on what is important. We no longer trust those leaders whose motives we are unsure of, or whose speeches contain only what they think we want to hear. Immediately, our suspicion is alerted, and their leadership effectiveness is significantly diluted.

As a leader, you must be able to stand up with confidence in three different areas:

1. **Stand up for:** This may be standing up for yourself, your values, or something you truly believe in or are passionate about. Good leaders are those who stand

up for what they believe and act on those convictions. They may not always win, but you know where they stand and what they stand for.

2. **Stand up with:** This is about standing up with your people – your teams, your customers, your stakeholders and your community. When you stand up with people, you show that you're 'on their side' when they need help. This builds long-term loyalty, trust, credibility, commitment and morale, and gives your people a confidence boost. It also shows that you are focused on your team's wellbeing and interests, rather than on yourself. This helps to create a positive working environment and shows everyone that you're a leader worth following.

3. **Stand up against:** This is about standing up against that which you disagree with or cannot tolerate. This means refusing to go along with or turn a blind eye to differences, even in the face of significant pressure to do so. Standing up against something is perhaps the riskiest element of all; however, it's one of the most powerful.

❙❙ Stop and reflect

Consider how you would rate yourself now in the three areas of standing for, with or against. Are you strong in one, or do you need help with all three?

How to stand strong

When it comes to building your confidence in standing strong, you have three areas to focus on:

1. **What do you VALUE?** Great leaders have strong beliefs about matters of principle. They have an unwavering commitment to a clear set of values and are passionate about their causes. People expect leaders to speak out on matters of values and conscience. To speak out, however, leaders have to know what to speak about. To stand up for their beliefs, they have to know what they stand for.

2. **What is your PURPOSE?** Steve Jobs once said, 'Being the richest man in the cemetery doesn't matter to me. Going to bed at night saying we've done something wonderful, that's what matters to me.' And Albert Einstein said, 'Nothing truly valuable arises from ambition or from a mere sense of duty; it stems rather from love and devotion towards men and towards objective things.' Here are two people with a clear sense of purpose. They are clear about what they stand for and why, and you need to be too.

3. **How RESILIENT are you?** Inevitably, when we stand up as leaders, we are putting ourselves at risk of rejection. Of course, at times we will be knocked down, and our confidence will wane. Building your capacity to get back up again is important in maintaining your confidence during adversity and setbacks. In other words, your resilience is key.

These three areas are highlighted in figure 3.1, and the following sections look at each in a little more detail.

Figure 3.1: Stand up

Work out your values and worth

Lieutenant General David Lindsay Morrison AO was the first head of the Australian Army to take a public stand against the military's ingrained culture of gender discrimination. His 2013 video message, which famously ordered misbehaving troops to 'get out' if they couldn't accept women as equals, went viral. He emphasised that 'the standard you walk past, is the standard you accept'. Morrison's values of inclusion and respect led him to take a very clear stand on inappropriate behaviour in the military, and this in turn led to him being awarded Australian of the Year in 2016.

The values that form the basis for your leadership come from your deeply ingrained beliefs and convictions. Of course, listing your values and living by them is easy when things are going well. I can do a values exercise with a group of leaders in half an hour and they can come up with a pretty clear list on what values are core to them. Only when your leadership, your success or your career is under pressure do you truly learn what is most important to you.

When you define your values, you lay the foundation for a grounded and confident leadership approach. You determine what matters most to you and you establish a framework by which you make decisions. Until leaders become clear in their own minds about what they value, becoming clear to others about what matters most is virtually impossible.

By defining your values, you allow your team members, your clients – and, most importantly, yourself – to know what you stand for.

Your values set you apart from other leaders.
Your values are what make you unique.

Personally, one of my core values is trust. So, as a leader, being able to have a strong foundation of trust in all of my relationships is vitally important. This is the basis for my connection with my people, and my stakeholders, colleagues and clients. In the past, when I worked in environments lacking trust, I took a stand against this, which has resulted in different outcomes at different times. On one occasion, I chose to leave a job because I knew developing trust to the level I needed wasn't possible. Being clear on trust as a core value of mine has given me the confidence to stand up for what I believe and lead in a way that is congruent with this value.

Knowing what motivates you is key to uncovering your values and when you are likely to be more or less confident. When it comes to motivation theory, psychologist Abraham Maslow's hierarchy of needs (from the 1940s) is the best known in the world. Maslow's idea was that people are first motivated by satisfying lower-level needs such as the need for food, water, shelter and security. Once these needs are satisfied, they can move on to being motivated by satisfying higher-level needs such as the need for self-actualisation and creativity.

While modern research shows some shortcomings with this theory, we can use Maslow's hierarchy of needs as a simple tool to assess our own motivators and apply these to our values.

Stop and reflect

Think about what motivates you – is it a need for security, such as being satisfied you have a nice place to live? Is it a need for family, and the feeling of being loved? Or are you motivated by feeling and being recognised and respected for your talents, perhaps?

When you look at what motivates you, how many of these are based on intrinsic motivations? *Intrinsic* motivations come from how you feel within and these provide fulfilment for far longer than *extrinsic* motivations, which come from measuring your success against the outside world's parameters and against how others might perceive you. Overall, moving away from extrinsic motivators and towards intrinsic ones leads to more sustainable – in other words, real – leadership confidence.

Once you've got a good view of your motivators, dig a bit deeper to understand how this translates to your values. What does it reveal about what you value deeply in life?

Be clear on your 'why'

Discovering your purpose is getting a lot of press right now. In times of disruption, and in organisations in particular, knowing *why* you are doing something can make you stand out from the pack – because it's not what you do, but how you do your job and, most importantly, why you do it that matters.

Your leadership purpose is yours and yours alone and comes from what you are driven to achieve as a leader. While you may express your purpose in different ways and contexts, it is what everyone close to you would recognise as uniquely you. It is your identity; the essence of who you really are. Your purpose doesn't have to be aspirational, cause-based or a result of who you think you should be. It comes from who you can't help being.

The problem with purpose is that you can feel pressured to be doing something to help make the world a better place. But it's actually a lot simpler than that. Think of a leader you have grown to respect or admire. Perhaps it is someone who inspires you. What was their leadership purpose? Was this purpose clear to you in the issues they took a stand on? Did they have the confidence to stand up for this purpose and follow through with their ideas? What impact did it have on them? What impact did it have on others?

What's the one thing that puts a fire in your belly? I was recently inspired and energised by my visit to Golden Door, a health retreat in the New South Wales Hunter Valley. During my visit, general manager Brigid lived and breathed wellbeing. She clearly lived an authentic and integrated life, and this lifestyle and philosophy was extended to her staff.

I couldn't help but notice their strong culture and leadership, with everything being aligned and on purpose. It was obvious that their values and beliefs were reflected in their actions. All the conversations they engaged in, how they looked and how they chose to relate to people spoke *wellbeing*. My interactions with them made me feel good, special, looked after and energised. Consequently, my experience as a client was one of complete trust. I knew Brigid and her team had my best interests at heart and I was able to immerse myself in the experience. That is purpose at its best.

Develop resilience

Your purpose is often discovered through the process of trying new things – and often through failing. Confidence is built in the same way. Waiting for things to be absolutely perfect before trying something new is *not* a formula for success.

Remember, the first book in JK Rowling's *Harry Potter* series was rejected 12 times before being signed up by a publisher. Murder mystery writer Agatha Christie was told 'no' continuously for five years before landing her first book deal. (Sales for her books are now estimated to be in excess of $2 billion.) And Walt Disney was once fired because his editor felt he lacked imagination and had no good ideas!

Can you imagine what would have happened if these iconic authors and creators had been overcome with self-doubt? Rejection is part of the journey, and a great leader will use past negative experiences to reframe and give meaning and purpose to their lives in terms of how they can lead. Instead of playing the victim, they will look for the inspiration within their life stories and use it to propel themselves forward and benefit others.

Developing your resilience as a leader is particularly important when you are:

- standing up for what you believe in;
- standing up with your team and supporting them to achieve something that felt out of reach;
- voicing an opinion that is against the majority;
- speaking up when no-one else will;
- leading change; and
- making unpopular decisions.

Ultimately, developing resilience is important when you need the confidence to believe in yourself as a leader.

Your true grit as a leader is shown not in how you perform or how confident you are in the good times, but rather in how you display strength, composure and confidence during the most challenging times. Demonstrating resilience is impossible unless you have experienced challenging times. Indeed, challenges and even traumas pose as an opportunity for further understanding and for recognising your deeper purpose as a leader.

So how do you maintain confidence and keep standing up for what you believe in, especially when things get tough?

Resilient leaders are confident in their own abilities. They focus on what they do well rather than what they struggle with, and they celebrate their achievements. They learn from success as much as failure, and this growth enhances their sense of confidence and resilience.

I love how Cindy Batchelor, Executive General Manager of NAB Business, talked about resilience in an interview with me:

> For me, resilience is the ability to bounce back. Life often throws challenges our way, and having the mental and physical strength to get back on track quickly is so important. This is about looking after yourself in the good times so when the going gets tough, you can reframe to positivity and move on. One of the things that Andrew Thorburn [CEO of NAB] and I have spoken about often is resilience because the more senior you become in an organisation, the more resilient you need to be. Leaders cast long shadows and others will look to you for strength through adversity.

Psychologist Martin Seligman is widely considered the founding father of the positive psychology movement and has spent years researching resilience. In his book *Learned Optimism*, Seligman proposes that our ability to deal with setbacks and to bounce back is largely determined by 3Ps and how we talk to ourselves in relation to them. The 3Ps are:

1. **Permanence:** This relates to how long we think a negative event or feeling will last. Do we see an event as stable or unstable? Someone with negative self-talk around permanence may use exaggeration in his or her thinking – for example, that 'this always happens' or 'I will always feel like this'. This kind of thinking might occur when you are so stressed that you wonder if you will ever not feel this way, or feel there is no light at the end of the tunnel. A confident leader, however, will think of the event differently and acknowledge that it's temporary while focusing on what the situation will look like once the problem has resolved.

2. **Pervasiveness:** This concerns the degree in which we generalise the negative circumstances and results from a specific event. A more negative belief, for example, would be that one setback will spread to all aspects of your life. A simple question might be to ask whether you are making mountains out of molehills. Someone with negative self-talk might interpret a single failure to mean that this will be the case everywhere, whereas a confident leader would contain the negative event to that specific situation and focus on what could be done better next time.

3. **Personalisation:** This is the degree to which you blame yourself, someone else or external factors for the negative event, and relates to the internalisation of failure. A person with negative self-talk may think, *It's all my fault*, whereas someone with more positive thinking is likely to acknowledge the various factors that contributed to the situation. Blaming yourself is easy when something negative happens, but doing this constantly wears you down. Negative self-talk here can result in a loss of self-esteem and confidence.

Understanding and referring to the 3Ps can be a terrific resource to use next time you're feeling like your confidence is low. Thinking in these terms can put everything into perspective and enhance your self-awareness. By acknowledging your feelings and how you got there, you can make more sense of the situation and can progress with more confidence and clarity. This will help you to build your resilience. Just remind yourself to acknowledge the 3Ps to get some perspective to see what is *really* going on.

> *What we tell ourselves about any event impacts on how we feel. This determines how resilient we are to endure the adversity and, therefore, how confident we are likely to remain.*

How much water can you carry?

Think about all of the different roles you play in your life – at work, at home, with family and with friends. Your roles might be as a partner, parent, employee, employer, mentor, sponsor, leader and/or community leader, for example. And as a result of those roles, you can identify the people you feel responsible for, and potentially even feel responsible for standing up for.

Imagine you are carrying a bucket of water on your head, as you might do if you were in Africa and had walked a long way to get water back to your village. The bucket can only hold so much water. Now imagine that each role we play and how much we stand up for the people we feel responsible for adds more water to that bucket.

If you're carrying too much water, it will spill out of the bucket and you will lose your ability to stand up with confidence.

This is exactly what happened to a client of mine. She was leading a major transformation program across her teams and, as a result, was restructuring roles and cutting jobs. Many of her direct reports, who had been in their roles for lengthy periods of time, had different perspectives on how the restructure should be implemented.

My client was getting so tied up in knots trying to represent all of their different views that she lost her own point of view. She tried to stand up for everyone, when in fact she really needed to back herself and have the confidence to stand up for what she was leading. When she realised what an impact trying to represent everyone was having on her, her business and the change, she started to stand up for herself with confidence and clarity. As a result, things turned around.

Stop and reflect

Think about how much water you can carry, and ask yourself:

- ► What roles are you playing and are these sustainable and effective?
- ► How many people are you standing up for?
- ► Are you represented in the bucket?
- ► Is your bucket about to overflow?
- ► What can you do to lessen the load?

Reviewing how much water you are carrying on a regular basis will help you be more thoughtful about who and what you are standing up for.

Knowing what you stand up for is at the heart of your leadership

In chapter 1, I mention my admiration for NASA Flight Director Gene Kranz and his work with the Apollo 13 mission. But Kranz had already experienced the worst-case scenario before Apollo 13. On 27 January 1967, Apollo 1 astronauts Gus Grissom, Ed White, and Roger Chaffee died in a fire during a training exercise. Following this, Kranz addressed his team, delivering what became known as the Kranz Dictum.

In this speech, Kranz acknowledged that, somewhere along the line, they screwed up. The mistake – whether it was in design, construction or testing – should have been caught, but it wasn't. They were too 'gung-ho' about pushing the schedule and getting into space, and no-one stood up and said stop. This was now Kranz's moment to stand up. He said,

From this day forward, Flight Control will be known by two words: 'tough' and 'competent.' Tough means we are forever accountable for what we do or what we fail to do. We will never again compromise our responsibilities. Every time we walk into Mission Control we will know what we stand for. Competent means we will never take anything for granted. We will never be found short in our knowledge and in our skills. Mission Control will be perfect. When you leave this meeting today you will go to your office and the first thing you will do there is to write 'tough and competent' on your blackboards. It will never be erased. Each day when you enter the room these words will remind you of the price paid by Grissom, White and Chaffee. These words are the price of admission to the ranks of Mission Control.

Kranz's words show what he was prepared to stand up for. His desire for honesty, purpose and perfection was at the heart of his leadership. What is at the heart of your leadership?

Check your confidence

1. When was the last time you stood up for what you believed in? How did it make you feel?

2. How would you rate your ability to stand up in the three areas: for, with and against? Are you strong in one area or do you need to work on all three?

3. What motivates you in life? What do you truly value? Are any of these extrinsic motivators that may need reassessing?

4. Think of a leader who you respect and admire. What is their leadership purpose? Think of a time when they stood up for what they believed in. How did that make you feel? What impact did it have on others?

5. What is the one thing that really puts a fire in your belly? How can you tap into that more often?

6. How resilient would you say you are on a scale of 1 to 10, with 10 being extremely resilient?

7. Reflect on the 3 Ps mentioned earlier in this chapter. How do you manage setbacks in terms of these three areas? What new strategies could you adopt using the 3Ps to increase your resilience?

8. How much water are you carrying? Do you need to set down your load and perhaps even get some help?

How did you find all the information in this chapter? Was it confronting, even a little scary? Good. That means you are already starting to build your confidence. No-one said this would be easy, and you have to go outside your comfort zone to really see some results. In chapter 4, we're going to take this even further – looking at how we speak up.

CHAPTER 4
SPEAK UP

Before we get into the 'guts' of this chapter, let's consider three different types of leaders. First, there's Brad – the type of experienced leader who is very focused on his results and is committed to getting the job done. Yet Brad has never been promoted beyond middle management. He always shows up just that little bit late to meetings and runs in rushed and out of breath. While he knows his stuff, he always looks a bit unsure of himself when put under any sort of pressure. He struggles to get his words out and, when he does, everyone in his meetings looks bored and uninterested.

Then there is Karen. She had been promoted rapidly over a shorter career, but all of a sudden seems to have stalled. She has been on succession plans for many senior leadership roles, but lately her more confident peers seem to be promoted over her. Like Brad, Karen is great at delivery in her role; however, when she speaks, she is hesitant and uses her hand to cover her mouth. She seldom makes eye contact and glances nervously up at the ceiling as she talks to executives.

Maria, on the other hand, is a mere five feet tall, yet when she enters a room and starts speaking she oozes passion for what she does and exerts confidence in her ability. People immediately sit up and listen. She remains composed under pressure and executes with a calmness that makes her respected among her many peers and executives. Even though she may have had some nerves about taking on a new and somewhat riskier senior leadership role, she didn't let that stop her stepping into it.

The difference between Brad, Karen and Maria is that Maria has the confidence to speak up.

Leadership means you must speak up.

Having the confidence to speak up is critical in leadership and is the essence of our work. As leaders, we are paid to have a voice, and to use that voice effectively and have a positive impact in our organisations. A sure way to fail in today's demanding business environment is to keep quiet when you should be speaking up!

Leaders often tell me that they don't speak up because they are not confident and they fear being judged. My response is, 'So you would rather be judged on just sitting there and saying nothing instead of taking the opportunity to have a voice and potentially getting it wrong?' The likelihood is that we are going to be judged one way or another.

Stop and reflect

How many of the following have you told yourself? You don't speak up because:

- You don't think you will be taken seriously.
- You're not sure how to say what you want to say.
- You don't feel you have anything really valuable to contribute.
- What's being discussed is not your area of expertise.
- You feel you would only be speaking for speaking sake.
- You're not sure how to break into the conversation so you'll raise your points later.
- You feel like what you want to ask is a stupid question.
- People will think you're an idiot.
- You don't want to cause conflict.

Remember – having the confidence to speak up is not about having an absence of fear. Having the confidence to speak up is the willingness to speak up in spite of the fear.

Power problems

What I have noticed over many years working with leaders is that confidence to speak up is more an issue when you question your power – that is, when you feel a loss of power or when you give your power away.

This generally plays out in two ways: firstly, in more senior meetings or forums or when working with more senior leaders; secondly, when stepping up into a more senior leadership role for the first time. In your first leadership role, you begin being thrown into internal and external meetings representing your business. At the executive level you start reporting into a board of many stakeholders. When you make it to CEO, you are the face and front of the whole organisation, and sometimes even the community. At each new level, your confidence and the ability to speak up can be challenged; however, your performance and your voice in these types of meetings matter a great deal – perhaps more than you think.

Feedback I often hear from clients is that they feel their voices are ignored or drowned out. Others tell me that they apologise repeatedly for what they are about to say before they even say it. Sometimes they have a hard time making their otherwise strong voices heard in meetings, either because they're not speaking loudly enough or because they can't find a way to break into the conversation at all. Even when they do find their way into the conversation, they fail to articulate a strong point of view. The questioning of their power affects their confidence which, in turn, has an impact on their ability to effectively speak up.

I also see leaders backing away from speaking up to avoid conflict. They see conflict as bad, rather than being able to reframe it as healthy debate. As a result, they keep their opinions to themselves – thinking that if they just keep doing their job and delivering the outcomes, they will get ahead.

That can work as a pretty good strategy for a while but, as you can see from the Brad and Karen examples, it only works for so long.

Leaders must be willing to speak up, even when it is hard or unpopular or you feel like it will cause conflict. As Martin Luther King Jr put it, 'Our lives begin to end the day we become silent about the things that matter'.

Don't ask, don't get

Julie, a client of mine (name changed), was going for her first general management role and wasn't completely confident in her ability. She suffered from a bit of 'imposter syndrome' (which I cover in more detail in chapter 5), so was thrilled when she found out she was successful in the role – that was, until the contract came.

She was immediately disappointed with the remuneration but, at first, thought she should just accept it and perhaps try for an increase somewhere down the track. She spoke about this approach with a couple of trusted colleagues. They disagreed, and gave her support, guidance and encouragement to have a conversation with her potential new employer.

She was very nervous about the prospect of this, but she prepared for the conversation by laying out all the facts. She thought about both the employer and her own needs, and what she thought was fair for both parties. She then stated her case and what she thought her value was and what she would be bringing to the new role.

After a further review, the new employer said yes to the proposed amount. Julie was shocked but very happy. Consequently, when she started her new role at the organisation, she was more ready and able to be engaged, and she felt equal to her peers.

She was proud of herself for having the confidence to negotiate a better outcome and speak up.

Time to speak

It was Eleanor Roosevelt who once said, 'You gain strength, courage and confidence by every experience in which you really stop to look fear in the face ... You must do the thing you think you cannot do.'

That means you've got to learn to speak up!

Speaking up involves developing three things:

1. Voice
2. Presence
3. Impact.

These three aspects are highlighted in figure 4.1, and discussed further in the following sections.

Figure 4.1: Speak up

Find your voice

Your voice is everything when it comes to being a leader. How you speak will affect how people listen to you.

Six steps are involved in finding your voice, as explored here.

Prepare to speak

To be able to perform properly in meetings, and to be able to speak up effectively, you need to prepare before the meeting. The issue is that most of us rush from one meeting to the next, with no time to reflect on how we want to speak up.

You need to slow down and think about your contribution and how you might have a real impact. You need to have prepared some notes that you want to talk about to allow yourself the ability to speak spontaneously.

When you prepare and come to a meeting with an accurate sense of what it's really about and how it will probably unfold, you can build on others' remarks. And you are better able to put forward your own point of view succinctly and with composure.

Maintain your tone

How you say what you say is crucial. People ask questions when they are seeking information or wanting approval for an idea or decision. While nothing is wrong with either of those situations, both can make you sound like you're questioning yourself if you are actually trying to make a point.

To project your voice with confidence, don't let the pitch of your voice creep upward at the end of a sentence. Maintain an even tone and finish your statements with full stops, not question marks.

As a Queenslander, I used to have a sing-a-long tone in my voice and tended to end a sentence with a question mark. I had a great sponsor early in my leadership career who gave me this feedback and caused me to tweak my tone. Doing so made a lot of difference to how others perceived my confidence.

Check your speed

Carmine Gallo, business communication expert and author of *Talk Like TED: The 9 Public-Speaking Secrets of the World's Top Minds*, claims 190 words per minute is the ideal speech speed for public speaking. At this speed, your audience will feel less like you're talking at them and more like you're having a conversation over lunch.

If you speak too slowly, you run the risk of putting your audience to sleep. And if you talk too quickly, you can sound amateurish or nervous, and as if you're trying to get the presentation over with as quickly as you can.

However, as you know, people speak at different rates at different times. If being nervous makes you speak faster, you need to be very conscious about slowing down. If you want to create some real energy in the room, you might want to think about speeding up. Your emotional state can greatly influence your speaking so it's important to be aware of that.

A simple way to calculate your speech rate is to record yourself using your mobile device that can convert your speech to text. Just talk for a couple of minutes and capture the text. Then cut and paste the text into a Word document and do a word count!

Use silence

Most of us fear silence when we are speaking. We rush to finish our point of view because we're worried we will be interrupted and won't get it all out. Or we think we might forget an important idea or lose our train of thought midway through a sentence. But silence isn't your enemy; it can actually be a powerful confidence-projecting tool.

Storytelling expert, author and colleague Gabrielle Dolan teaches leaders that audiences need strategic pauses in order to retain and understand important points. Additionally, the ability to live with silences, whether of your own making or the audience's, makes you seem more confident.

Watch your language

Do you ever begin your sentences with words or phrases such as, 'This is just my opinion', 'Sorry', 'I'm still working on this', 'Well', 'I mean' or any number of other negative prefaces?

Most people use these as a matter of habit or nervousness, but caveats and fillers can damage the confident tone you're trying to strike. Instead, say what you mean and nothing else. For example, 'We should take this pitch in a different direction,' is much more persuasive than, 'Well, I think we should take this pitch in a different direction, but I'm still trying to find out the best route to take.'

Try the opposite

I had a woman on a leadership program tell me about her tactic for speaking up in meetings. She referred to the *Seinfeld* episode 'The Opposite' where George returns from the beach and decides that every decision that he has ever made has been wrong, and so his life is the exact opposite of what it should be.

George tells this to Jerry, who convinces him that 'if every instinct you have is wrong, then the opposite would have to be right'. George then resolves to start doing the complete opposite of what he would do normally.

My client realised that normally she would sit back in meetings and listen, and very often walk out having never spoken. She found that by using 'the opposite' as a fun tactic, she could find her voice early in meetings. She found that when she started to see evidence of this working successfully, she built confidence – and it just kept growing from there.

Develop your presence

As a leader, you are constantly being evaluated on how well you display confidence, composure, credibility and connection. Your presence, or lack thereof, can make all the difference in terms of how you are perceived.

Although leadership presence is hard to define, it is not some innate quality that you either have or have not. It is a set of learned behaviours that enables you to command attention. When you are fully present, you inspire others.

Ultimately, your leadership presence is your ability to project self-confidence, exercise leadership in different contexts, make tough decisions as required and hold your own with other leaders. Which behaviours signal your presence to others? And how do you improve your presence? The following sections provide some ideas.

Get feedback

Engage a few trusted colleagues who will give you honest feedback on what you are projecting. Tell them you are trying to build your level of leadership presence and would like specific feedback on how you are coming across in different forums.

Remember the three YOUs from chapter 2 and the importance of understanding how you are being perceived by others. If you're a leader, the simple fact is this: others' perception of you is your reality. Whatever perception people have of your leadership effectiveness creates the reality you're operating in.

#ownit

Gabrielle Dolan, Jac Phillips and I coined the term '#ownit' when we travelled to Harvard Kennedy School for their Women and Power program in 2016. We made a discovery that you can get yourself into the first class lounges in some airports if you looked like you belong. Approach with confidence, back up straight, smile and connect and in you walk!

Now it wasn't always as simple as that and it isn't always as simple as that in leadership either, but when you #ownit you do project a different presence. We all know people who do this well and the impact this has on their presence is tangible.

Focus

Research from as far back as 2001 shows clearly that leaders are operating under elevated strain, pressure and anxiety because of managing ever-increasing workloads during periods of rapid organisational and societal change. Add into that mix the pervasive impact of 24/7 connectivity and we have an even bigger problem.

For many leaders, their existence has become one of minimal downtime, constant interruptions to family life and a sense of never getting away from work. Our focus and attention being scattered, however, impacts on our presence. We are all over the shop! So how do we gain focus in the face of this competing need for attention?

Jon Kabat-Zinn is a professor emeritus of medicine and the creator of the Stress Reduction Clinic and the Center for Mindfulness in Medicine, Health Care, and Society at the University of Massachusetts Medical School. Kabat-Zinn strongly links focus and attention to mindfulness, and in *Wherever You Go, There You Are: Mindfulness Meditation in Everyday Life* says, 'The best way to capture moments is to pay attention. This is how we cultivate mindfulness. Mindfulness means being awake. It means knowing what you are doing.'

We need to have the ability to think clearly and to focus on what is most important at any given time. In his book *Focus: The hidden driver of excellence*, author and science journalist (mainly reporting on the brain and behavioural sciences) Daniel Goleman explains that the link between attention and excellence remains hidden most of the time. Yet attention is the basis of the most essential of leadership skills.

Being able to focus and give attention to what we are doing and who we are doing it with creates a much stronger connection. And with this connection comes a better leadership presence. When we are distracted and only give people half of our attention, trust and presence are eroded.

Check your body language

The body language that accompanies your message is just as important as the words coming out of your mouth. According to Carol Kinsey Goman, PhD, an executive coach and consultant in nonverbal communication, audiences perceive speakers to have more positive traits – such as warmth and energy – when they use a variety of gestures. While some physical gestures, such as fiddling with clothing or touching your hair, can distract or convey a lack of confidence, using your hands when you speak is a great way to communicate your excitement and knowledge about the topic.

Also try some of body language expert Amy Cuddy's 'power poses' before important meetings and speaking on stage. Get your Wonder Woman or Superman poses on (think chin high, arms strong) when preparing to encourage a stronger, more powerful posture and body language.

Breathe

Calm is the foundation of presence – a big ask for many leaders today. To maintain a peaceful centre, learn to use your breath as an awareness tool.

We can learn a lot from yogi philosophy on breathing, and its ability to help us create stillness even when the world around may be in chaos. We often talk about 'breathing easy' to show we are relaxed and have let go of a problem or worry. We use the term 'breathing room' when we need more space for sufficient air or to sort something out. And we express our understanding of breath when we advise someone who is angry to 'take 10 deep breaths' before they speak or act from anger. In fact, a period of quiet deep breathing causes blood pressure to drop – and to stay down for as long as 30 minutes – according to a study published in the *Journal of the American Geriatric Society*. How is that for calm!

Breathing is at the heart of virtually every meditation practice. This is because paying attention to the breath brings us fully into the present. It is impossible to focus on the breath without paying attention to the here and now. You can practise paying attention to your breath to create a calm, peaceful centre.

Have impact

Now you're ready to use your new confidence in your voice and your presence! Next, you need to speak up in a way that creates impact.

Thinking about how best to speak up for impact requires you to uncover some fundamental truths.

Firstly, why are you speaking? What are you contributing?

When I work with clients on speaking up, they often say to me that they don't want to be like that particular colleague who speaks up time and time again and just loves the sound of their own voice (you know the one). Becoming that person is not what this is about. Be thoughtful about why and how you are speaking up.

Secondly, how likely is it that others will share your purpose or what you are trying to have an impact on?

I have seen many leaders who have not spent enough time understanding this. When they then speak up, they are drowned out by stronger voices who all have an alternative view. Know what other perspectives exist. Spend time talking to key influencers and stakeholders to understand their point of view. This will help inform you about tactics or strategies for how you speak up and who you need to speak to.

This understanding will help you decide:

- Is a question or observation most useful?

- Should I provide some data to guide the discussion or draw in others to the discussion with the objective of getting like-minded stakeholders talking to each other?
- Do I need to raise the heat in the meeting by challenging behaviour or bringing conflict to the surface to make progress?

A well-targeted intervention takes thought, preparation and confidence. It is likely to incorporate at least two or three of the principles set out in table 4.1, which outlines a variety of actions and techniques to help you think about speaking up differently and effectively, depending on the context and the outcome you're seeking.

Perhaps the most difficult skill to develop is being able to judge how to best speak up and when and with what intensity. The answer to this question cannot be taught in any linear or routine way but rather develops through experience.

Observe and read the play, experiment with your approach and do not let fear limit you to only one way of speaking up.

The purpose	The practice
To get and hold people's attention	Use silence Use storytelling
To 'raise the heat'	Challenge or call out the behaviour Ask a hard question or propose an alternative idea Bring conflicts to the surface
To 'lower the heat'	Take responsibility back Praise and acknowledge Use humour
To delegate the work	Ask questions of the group: What do you need from me? What can you do?
To hold the mirror up	Ask questions of the group: How would we know if this has worked? What just happened in this conversation?
To orchestrate cross-party dialogue	Get factions talking to each other
To get people on the balcony	Observe what is going on Understand the bigger picture
To test the current reality	Ask yourself questions: What's the worst thing about that? What if that is a convenient story we are telling ourselves?
To understand the facts	Ask fact-based questions of the group or individuals: Who is involved? What are the relationships?

Table 4.1: Purpose and practice

A 'Virgin voice'

Janelle Hopkins is the Group CFO at Australia Post. She reached this position through hard work and truly earning her seat at the executive table. She was excited to be invited to a lunch with Richard Branson when he was in Australia for the World Forum.

'I was thinking it would be 200 people' she told me. 'When I walked in it was literally 20 people around a table having lunch with Branson, and I was sitting one seat away from him. Literally one away from him! I thought, *Oh, my God. I've got to sound smart. What can I say?*'

When she took a moment to reflect, she realised that as the CFO of one of Australia's biggest companies she had plenty to say. 'I started to think, *Wow, what a fabulous opportunity.* What was really important for me was to come to the party with something insightful to say. I didn't want to sit there and not say anything.'

Janelle believes as leaders we are paid to have a point of view. This is not about proving ourselves as leaders but exercising leadership by having a voice.

Check your confidence

1. How often do you fail to speak up out of fear of being judged, or as a way of avoiding conflict? What would happen if you started to change that today? How would you feel? How would it affect your overall leadership influence?

2. In what situations do you struggle most to speak up? For example, during team meetings or social events?

3. The next time you are at a meeting, event or whatever you outlined in answering the preceding question, follow the

six steps to find your voice: prepare to speak, maintain your tone, check your speed, use silence, watch your language and try the opposite. What do you notice as a result? What are you strong at? What could you work more on?

4. Get some feedback on your current presence. Ask a handful of trusted colleagues or friends to give you honest feedback on what you are projecting to others. What do you notice? What surprises you? What do you need to work on? Remember, this is about getting some honest and valuable advice so you can take constructive next steps to speak up. This is not an exercise to make you feel bad or lower your confidence further.

You are now one more stage down in the Confidence Model, with just one more area to cover. Next, we'll explore how you step up your confidence and leadership. This is where you will really start tapping into your true potential – so read on to chapter 5.

CHAPTER 5
STEP UP

David, a former client of mine (name changed) was struggling with a sense of deep frustration. 'I've worked really hard my entire career,' he would say. 'I have delivered performance above and beyond expectations consistently. I receive great performance reviews every year. My 360-degree feedback reports are about the best going around. I am always taking on additional work by way of mentoring others and contributing to projects outside of my scope. I've even moved cities twice so they know I am mobile. I do community work and help others in their career. But in the last year I've been passed over twice for promotion. Why?'

Does this scenario sound familiar?

Unfortunately, this is all too common in senior management. I've met countless leaders like David throughout my career who are exceptional performers and yet continue to miss out on promotions and have limited understanding of why.

These leaders are frustrated at not making sufficient progress or getting the level of results they are seeking. They are feeling beaten up; they are working really long hours and for what? Their lack of progress is because they are *working and leading as they always have.*

You need to learn to step up and exercise leadership differently at each new level in your leadership journey. You need to have the confidence and skills, and the ability to take on an element of risk. To step up confidently, you need to master your mindset, build your personal brand and have great sponsors.

In my time with him, David did a lot of work to understand what he really wanted from his career. He focused on building his confidence every day, and really stepping into it and owning it. He moved from struggling to have any influence in his organisation to making a real impact. He started to really believe he had it in him to take on senior and executive roles. He found a couple of great sponsors and started to ask for what he wanted.

Consequently, David was offered the opportunity to take on a general management role and is now well on his way to executive roles. When I talk to him today about that time, he can hardly recognise himself because he has changed so much.

Build the confidence to step up your leadership performance, impact, influence and, ultimately, in readiness for your next leadership role.

Challenging your behaviour

In 2007, leadership coach Marshall Goldsmith published *What Got You Here Won't Get You There*. The essence of Goldsmith's book is that many of the behaviours that initially propel high-achievers up the corporate ladder are paradoxically the same ones preventing them from reaching the very top.

He talks about habits like winning too much (for example, the need to win every workplace disagreement, even when it doesn't matter), adding too much value (adding your two cents to every discussion) and goal obsession (becoming so wrapped up in achieving short-term goals that you forget the larger mission). These habits are no longer required when you really want to step up as a leader.

You may well have been recognised for behaviours early in your career that demonstrated you were driven, but the moment you step into a position of leadership, these behaviours become counterproductive.

Leadership is about much more than demonstrating the single-minded drive to get the work done. This drive shows you can 'do' the work but it does not demonstrate that you are a leader.

As a leader, reflecting on your current leadership behaviours and stepping up as required is critical. You often need to lead differently tomorrow from how you lead today. You need to take yourself out of your comfort zone – and be confident enough to do this – and be aware of your context and what the environment requires of you to lead because this is always changing. Continue to challenge yourself and ask, 'If what got me here won't get me there, what do I need to be doing now to step up?'

Doing things differently often means stepping *away* from many of the day-to-day 'doing' tasks of your job. It means not only leading your own business team or business unit, but also exercising leadership and influence across your peers and upwards in your organisation. If you've got your 'head down and bum up' all day long, knocking off items on your to-do list, how will you be able to assess what you need to do to influence and ensure the work makes real progress? Looking higher and wider means learning to delegate to the team who is doing the work, which can be scary.

We tell ourselves comforting stories when we fear letting go of control and putting our trust in others – telling ourselves not enough resources are available, for example, or the team doesn't have the right capability. Or we say it's not the right time yet, and we can do it quicker and better ourselves. Telling yourself stories such as these can be really damaging because you need to develop the confidence to step up and exercise leadership differently.

Cindy Batchelor, Executive General Manager of NAB Business, regularly reflects on how she exercises leadership and influence in her role:

> Leadership is a journey. For first-time leaders or those early in their career, focusing on performance in your own business is a sensible thing to do. Setting clear goals, inspiring your people and delivering performance works well – and is all pretty straightforward. Or is it? This is easy to say but much harder to do. In reality, linear leadership doesn't really exist in organisations. Even if you run a business area or are the most senior person in your unit, you then become a member of a more senior team and need to have an impact in the next 'level up'.
>
> So how do you get members of teams contributing for the whole rather than just their own business unit? I call it 'level-up leadership'. Today in my national NAB Business role, I spend 50 per cent of my time on my business and 50 per cent of my time on enterprise initiatives. This also creates space for people in my team to 'step up' and lead in my absence – a great development opportunity for all. Influencing outside your role is harder than when you hold positional leadership but it is the true test of leadership – can you influence without total control?

Work it

Mark (name changed) had just been promoted to his first general manager role, and he was tasked with recruiting a new team that would enable him to step up and lead at a different level. The problem was, he struggled to let go and kept thinking he could still do all the work.

This meant he didn't put enough emphasis on bringing the right level of talent into the team. Even when he did get the right people on board, he still kept working at their level because it was what he was familiar with – this was where he felt safe.

He wasn't stepping up and putting himself out there. He was afraid of failing and didn't think he had what it took to lead at the next level up.

Mark was lucky to be working for a fantastic leader at the time, who took him under his wing and gave him some feedback about his performance.

Knowing he had someone in his corner, Mark then started to contribute more in senior forums. He started to understand that leadership looked different at this next level up.

He engaged me as his coach so he could work on the behavioural change he needed to really step up. He started to believe in himself as he tried new ways of leading and his mindset shifted to one of confidence as he stepped into his new role and identity.

Imposing feelings

Janelle Hopkins (currently Group CFO at Australia Post) had just turned 30 when she got her first senior role as financial controller. She had a team of 50 people and was presenting to boards – all while being, at the time, the youngest person in the room. When I spoke to Janelle about this experience she said:

> I thought, *What the hell am I doing here? They're going to find out soon that I don't really know all this stuff.* I would be afraid to express an opinion to my more senior peers because I would feel as if they had much more experience.

A lot of the time, I was the only woman in the room with lots of 50-year-old men.

At this time, Janelle suffered from 'impostor syndrome'. This term was first coined by psychologists Pauline Rose Clance and Suzanne Imes in 1978. Their research showed that, despite outstanding achievements, the participants in their study did not experience any internal feeling of success. They put these achievements down to luck and believed themselves to be 'frauds' or 'impostors'.

Imposter syndrome impacts our confidence and limits our ability to step up our leadership.

Numerous doctoral theses and research papers have followed Clance and Imes's original study. Although the findings from these follow-up studies have not always been consistent, most studies suggest that these imposter feelings are not limited to just women and up to 70 per cent of people experience impostor syndrome at some stage in their career.

Characteristics of imposter syndrome include:

- ► feeling you do not deserve your current success or position;
- ► believing it is only a matter of time before people find out that you do not know what you are doing;
- ► thinking you have obtained your position by mistake – many of the students Clance and Imes researched believed it was the result of an administrative error;

- attributing your success to luck – for example, that you were in the 'right place at the right time'; and

- downplaying and discounting any success you achieve – 'I was just the best of a bad bunch' or 'It was nothing, anyone could have done it'.

These thoughts can cause real problems for you as a leader because you are:

- reluctant to take on new responsibilities, projects or promotions as you feel you are 'not quite' ready;

- quick to be risk averse due to fear of failure;

- unable to celebrate successes or even talk about successes, which can have a negative impact on promotions, personal brand and other opportunities;

- reactive to negative feedback or even constructive criticism, which can lead to unprofessional behaviour and limited growth; and

- stressed and anxious due to the constant worry of being found out.

Your ability to master your self-talk, therefore, is the first place to start your journey of stepping up.

Start to step up

There are three elements to stepping up:

1. Mastering your mindset
2. Re-branding yourself
3. Building sponsorship.

These three elements are highlighted in figure 5.1 and discussed in the following sections.

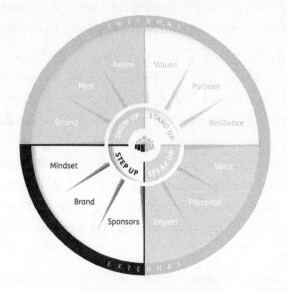

Figure 5.1: Step Up

Master your mindset

The way we talk to ourselves determines how we think, with positive self-talk leading to a positive mindset. Occasionally, I come across someone who asks me, 'So, what is self-talk, really?'

Self-talk is the commentary that we have going on in our heads. It's our inner voice, and what we say to ourselves that we often don't say out loud.

If our self-talk is positive, we generally feel good about ourselves. Our internal thoughts are saying good things about us and our life and this often makes us more optimistic about the possibilities in our life. If our self-talk is negative, however, we can feel pretty bad about ourselves, and this cycle can be very self-defeating. In fact, if our inner voice is consistently critical and harsh, the effect can be crippling.

While much debate is still occurring in this space, most experts recognise that the average person has somewhere between 50,000 and 70,000 thoughts per day. That's a lot of thinking! No wonder we go home tired some days. In fact, it's almost impossible to stop thinking. While the content and tone of our self-talk varies a lot from positive to negative, human nature is more prone to negative and repetitive self-talk. This means having tools and tactics to get on top of our negative self-talk and stay balanced in our thinking is critical.

In 'The executive mind: leader self-talk, effectiveness and strain' by Steven Rogelberg (Professor and Director of Organizational Science at the University of North Carolina Charlotte) and his university colleagues, Rogelberg outlines their investigation into the nature of self-talk among effective and ineffective managers. The authors concluded that 'constructive self-talk positively related to effective leadership of others'. The study also found the more you talk yourself down, second-guess yourself, and see changes as threatening, the less free your mind is to roam through creative solutions to the problems you face.

The good news is you can learn how to master your mindset and self-talk. Thinking negatively is really just a bad habit that you can change.

You have to start by paying attention to what is going on in your head. Notice what your inner voice is saying. What are the themes? When we are busy, operating on automatic pilot is easier and, therefore, we don't ever pause to notice our self-talk. Negative self-talk can spiral south quickly so developing the ability to listen and notice to yours is important.

When you notice negative self-talk, ask yourself a few simple questions:

► What are the facts?

► What would a trusted friend or colleague say?

► What's a more positive way to look at this?

The answers to these questions can help you to think about how to change or re-frame your self-talk to something more positive or at least neutral.

The following outline some negative examples of self-talk and how they can be reframed:

► **Negative:** I've never done something this big before; I'll probably stuff it up.

► **Re-frame:** I love a challenge. This assignment is simply a bigger version of what I've been successful at before. It's time to step up.

► **Negative:** I really don't think I could do that presentation to so many people. What if I fail so publicly?

► **Re-frame:** I know my stuff so I'll commit to doing it knowing I can do the necessary work to get ready for the big day.

It is not always easy to achieve a positive mindset, but it is critical in being able to see the possibilities of stepping up your leadership.

Stop and reflect

One of the simplest pieces of advice I give to my clients to improve their self-talk is to practise gratitude daily. At the end of every day, think about three things you have to be grateful for. This is a lovely exercise to do around the dinner table at night with your family. To make the process specific to imposter syndrome, you can tweak your gratitude exercise to reflect on three things you did well that day, or three pieces of positive feedback you received.

Just try it and see.

Challenge yourself

When I first started working with Allan (name changed) years ago, he had set the bar pretty low for himself in terms of what he wanted out of his career. He was in a middle management role and, when we had career conversations, he made it clear he definitely wasn't interested in executive roles.

Allan found it hard to articulate why that was the case. He was really good at getting the job done and was in his comfort zone when he was 'doing' the work. The thought of stepping up really freaked him out and he assumed he wouldn't be successful at executive level.

His negative self-talk and lack of belief in himself was holding him back. He had the skills, however, so together we started to challenge that self-talk.

He started to experiment with operating at more senior levels by taking on work that required more of an executive presence and more influence. He got good feedback, which encouraged him to do more of this type of work. As he stepped up and led differently, the positive momentum increased his confidence. He kept going, and going.

Today he is in an executive role and having the time of his life. When he reflects on how much he was holding himself back he puts it all down to confidence (or lack thereof).

Re-brand yourself

Oprah Winfrey, Richard Branson, Lady Gaga, Steve Jobs, Beyoncé and Sheryl Sandberg are all names that are thrown up when I ask my clients to think of people with a strong brand. Each of these celebrities and leaders is a master of personal branding. They haven't become famous by accident. They have put effort into defining their brand so we know what they stand for and what they are all about. Their personal brands have helped them manoeuvre in the business world (even if their fame comes from other areas) and become global success stories.

We often think of 'brand' in terms of companies and marketing or high-profile individuals and celebrities. But personal branding isn't just for the rich and famous. When you think about the high-performing leaders you know, chances are they will all have a strong, clear personal brand. In other words, you have a good sense of what they stand for.

Leaders with strong personal brands know how to leverage their strengths to create the best version of themselves. Let's look at Marissa Mayer, for example. According to brand strategist and author Laura Ries, Mayer created a strong brand as Google's 20th employee and first woman engineer. This helped her to then go on and become CEO of Yahoo.

As Jeff Bezos, founder and CEO of Amazon, says, 'Your brand is what people say about you when you are not in the room.'

Your personal brand is created by the experiences people have with you in all different contexts – whether that be face to face, online, the stories others share about you, your actions, your words or the way you dress. Not only that, but you create your brand the minute you walk into a room.

The real problem is that most of us, as leaders, don't take the time to invest in developing the right brand for what we want to achieve. A strong authentic brand should always be evolving, to help you stand out from the crowd and help you achieve professional and personal success.

Your personal brand must align to where you want to take your leadership and career; this is the only way your brand will support you stepping up. Your personal brand needs to support your future leadership roles as much as your current one. Again, you need to be always thinking about what you would like people to say about you when you're not in the room, and what is going to get you that next promotion or opportunity, and shape your personal brand around this.

Say your new role requires you to be influential, a strong negotiator, strategic and have great interpersonal skills but your current brand is more about being a good 'doer' and a quiet achiever, and seeing things a bit 'black-and-white'. In this situation you have work to do on your brand to enable you to step up your performance.

Stop and reflect

Personal branding isn't easy, but thinking through your unique strengths, your career goals and aspirations, and how you want others to perceive you over the next few years is a great first step.

Try the following and track your results:

- **Define what you want your brand to be.** What are the elements of the brand that you want for yourself? What is your point of difference? Think two to three years out to ensure your brand supports a stepped-up version of you. Make your brand clear and write it down.

- **Get feedback on what your current brand is.** Ask colleagues who know you well and you trust to give you honest feedback. A simple way to do this is to ask five people for five words that describe your current brand.

- **Make an action plan to build your desired brand based on that feedback.** Make an action plan to address the areas you want to work on, and then start consistently leading in a way that aligns to your new brand.

Oprah, Branson and all the rest never leave their personal brand to chance, so neither should you.

Six brand touch points

In terms of building out your brand, I love the work of Jane Anderson – an Australian specialising in personal branding. As part of what Anderson says about branding, she advises you to look at your visible branding touch points. Jane's main areas to focus on are:

1. How you dress
2. Where you sit
3. The state of your desk
4. Your slides for your presentation
5. Your verbal tone
6. Your attitude
7. Your eye contact.

Remember – every aspect of your behaviour and how people experience you affects your brand.

Consequently, reflecting on what you do that can negatively impact your brand is also important. Anderson outlines the following top five things as doing the most damage to your brand:

1. Not managing your Facebook page
2. Not managing your diary
3. Not filling out your LinkedIn profile fully
4. Dressing for your current job, rather than your future job
5. Not managing your 'first four seconds' – that is, the impression you make on others when you first meet them.

So take the time to re-brand you. Ensure your personal brand supports a stepped up, authentic, confident version of you, and one that you are excited and energised to step into. (For more of Jane's tips, see her book *Impact*.)

Build sponsorships – you can't do it on your own

Stepping up in your career and your leadership is not a lone activity and, as you go into more senior leadership roles, sponsorship is critical. A sponsor is someone who will give you the support and backing you need to be successful in your current role and in your ability to step up into more senior roles.

A sponsor's role is to advocate for you when and where you need to be more visible – they put your name forward for roles you did not know existed or were becoming vacant, for example. In fact, many senior roles are not even advertised, so you need sponsors advocating for you where you can't. A great sponsor will also help with your confidence because they will support you to step up when you might be holding yourself back.

Sponsors don't just magically appear. Sponsorship must be earned and reviewed on an ongoing basis. But when you have the right sponsor, the result can change your career.

It is important to have a system in place and be very conscious about what sponsorship you need to support your career and your leadership. Follow the four steps outlined in figure 5.2 to help with your sponsorship goals.

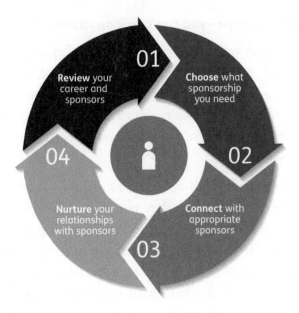

Figure 5.2: Getting sponsorship

Choose the sponsorship you need

Be strategic about the sponsorship you need and then search for would-be sponsors based on this. Look beyond your immediate circle of mentors and leaders. While you should, of course, impress your boss – who can be a valuable connection to potential sponsors – you should seek out someone with real power to support your career.

Would-be sponsors in large organisations are ideally two levels above you with line of sight to your role; in smaller firms, they're either the CEO or someone on the executive team.

Connect with appropriate sponsors

Have a conversation with potential sponsors. Don't leave it to chance and assume they will act as sponsor for you for a specific role you are applying for or more generally be opening doors for you just because you impressed them in some way in the past.

Nurture your relationships with sponsors

Like every good relationship, your sponsor relationship needs to be nurtured. How you build the relationship will likely look different for different sponsors, but it is important to be proactive about how you nurture and manage these relationships.

As a (bad) example of this, I had a leader call me who had worked for me some time ago. He wanted me to be a referee for a new role at executive level and said he would also like my sponsorship by way of supporting him into the role. I hadn't heard from him for eight years! I could barely remember his achievements. Nevertheless, I offered to provide a reference. But I didn't hear from him again for another nine months – at which point he told me he didn't get the job and asked whether I could sponsor him again. The answer was no!

Review your career and sponsors

Every 12 months, you must sit down and review your sponsorships. This is best performed at the same time as you are looking ahead to what you want to achieve for the year professionally and what development needs to take place to support that. Sponsors move in and out of organisations regularly so you never want to find yourself having applied for a role or needing support with no-one senior to advocate for you.

Finding the right people to be your sponsors and highlight your accomplishments is not always easy, but it is necessary. Just doing good work isn't enough.

Take the first step and make yourself not only a hard worker, but a leader who has stepped up and is worthy of sponsorship.

Would you sponsor me?

The following comes from my interview with Cindy Batchelor, Executive General Manager, NAB Business.

I've been very conscious about building advocacy through my career. I call it 'sponsorship' and here I'm referring to someone who is prepared to put their reputation on the line to recommend me. It is important to be deliberate and authentic – they must know you well, have experience of your capabilities and also your development needs, and be prepared to speak for you. Sponsors with influence are very powerful people in your arsenal of supporters.

Every 12 months or so I review my sponsor list and ask myself, for my next role, which people could be authentic sponsors for me. If people on my list have not had recent and relevant exposure to me, it may be time to add others to the list. It is also important to have honest conversations with potential sponsors to see if your aspirations align to their experience of your strengths and potential. In some cases, they would sponsor you for particular roles but not all roles. This is powerful and sobering information. You've got to be quite specific and not make assumptions because you might think you have a sponsor and that doesn't play out.

Check your confidence

1. What got you to where you are today? What do you need to do differently to get you to where you want to be tomorrow?

2. Do you ever suffer from imposter syndrome? Use the characteristics listed earlier in this chapter to help you analyse this. If any ring true, consider how your thoughts and feelings are holding you back, and whether this is an issue you need some professional help with.

3. How do you talk to yourself? Next time you hear yourself using negative self-talk, try writing down what you are saying and reframing it into something positive.

4. What is your current personal brand? What do you want it to be? Work through the three steps outlined in the 'Re-brand yourself' section to help you with this: define what you want your brand to be, get feedback on what your current brand is and make an action plan to build your desired brand based on that feedback.

5. What sponsors do you currently have? What sponsors do you need? What could you do today that will get you one step closer to finding or nurturing the right people around you?

You have now worked through the four areas of the Confidence Model: show up, stand up, speak up and step up. But your hard work doesn't just end here. As you know, confidence is not a set-and-forget activity. You need to constantly reassess and work on your confidence – and that's just what we'll do in part III.

PART III
LIVE

As you know by now, confidence is not a build-it-once-and-you-have-it-forever scenario. If only life were that simple! This is why confidence is a cycle, rather than a linear process. It's something you work on time and time again – building your confidence is the first part, but sustaining it is the second.

You need to regularly check in with yourself as you work on your confidence. You need to assess how confident you are at certain stages of your career, as well as in certain situations – such as during a negotiation, presentation or strategy you are developing.

I am generally a really confident person overall, for example, but *wow* did I see a different side to myself when I started writing this book!

When you assess your confidence, you can work out when your confidence is high and when it is low and work on making it more sustainable – and that is what we cover in the next chapters.

CHAPTER 6
DEAL WITH YOUR ENEMIES

Gary (name changed) has been a client of mine for many years. He is an authentic leader and does the work to show up as the best version of himself. He stands up for his team and his values. He has a strong voice and leadership presence, so speaks up effectively and has developed the ability to step up his leadership on an ongoing basis.

But every so often he has a real blow to his confidence that can affect his whole performance. A man who generally has no issues with confidence suddenly starts questioning his ability to do his job.

The enemies of confidence

The previous four chapters looked at the why, what and how of showing up, standing up, speaking up and stepping up your leadership with confidence. Yet there are five overarching elements that work against our confidence and affect our leadership potential, no matter where we are or how good we are feeling in a situation. Figure 6.1 shows these five 'enemies of confidence'.

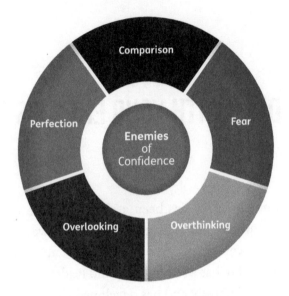

Figure 6.1: Enemies of confidence

Let's explore each enemy in turn to see how you can deal with them to make sure you strengthen your confidence if you find it wavering.

Perfection

Do you ever catch yourself saying something similar to the following:

► 'This paper I've written isn't good enough. I can't submit it like this.'

- 'Other people speak on this topic far better than I do; I won't volunteer to be the speaker this time.'

- 'I only have 7 of the 10 requirements for that more senior role. I won't apply for a promotion until I am perfectly ready.'

If any of these sound familiar to you, or your self-talk echoes the same ideas, then you may suffer from perfectionism. When you're a perfectionist, you refuse to do things unless they are done just right. You're unwilling to act unless what you do is guaranteed to win and to wow, absolutely without any chance of loss.

When your self-confidence is low, you hold yourself back, make limiting choices and give your power over to perfectionism.

Confidence is built on you accepting yourself and your abilities, and on you having a go and learning along the way. It is built on taking action and making progress and feeling great about that, and about not being afraid to fail.

So unless you can find a way to overcome your tendency for perfectionism, it will hold you back from doing anything new, different or challenging. As a leader, this may mean you never apply for that promotion, you never negotiate what you are really worth, you never put your hand up to sponsor that new project and, ultimately, you never really step up and reach your full leadership potential. You will fail to act and act to fail.

While perfectionism happens regardless of your gender, cultural background or experience, study after study indicates that women are more prone to it. Indeed, when I coach women, and even talk to girlfriends, I often find that we don't answer questions until we are totally sure of the answer, we don't submit an assignment (or publish a book!) until we've edited it *ad nauseam*, and we don't sign up for that fun run unless we know we are faster and fitter than is required. We watch our male colleagues take more risks, while we hold back until we're sure we are perfectly ready and perfectly qualified. We overthink our performance at home, at school, at work, at yoga class, and even on holiday. We obsess as mothers, wives, sisters, friends, cooks and athletes.

However, women are certainly not alone in facing this perfectionism challenge. Bob Sullivan and Hugh Thompson, experts in disruption and leadership and authors of *The Plateau Effect*, call this tendency the 'enemy of the good'. They explain that perfectionism can lead us all – men and women – to waste hours and hours of time. The irony is that striving to be perfect actually keeps us from getting much of anything done.

To overcome perfectionism, and build confidence, you need to act! It's only when you learn to let go and actually take action that you gain confidence, which breaks the cycle of perfectionism.

Firstly, you must acknowledge that you are human and, therefore, not perfect! If you've accepted that you make mistakes, when you make one, you can learn from it and move on quite quickly. (And if you're not making any mistakes, it's a sign that you are playing it too safe.)

Secondly, you need to develop a stronger self-belief. We put far more pressure on ourselves to be perfect than anyone else ever does or would. It's up to you to take the first step, and then a second step and so on. There's nothing like progress and momentum to help us along the way. Avoid the idea that you have to be 'all or nothing', because this gets you nowhere.

Thirdly, have someone in your support network who will give you honest feedback and call out if you are trying too hard to perfect something. Often, we are unable to see this in ourselves, and have some great stories to tell ourselves for why we aren't ready – we're not good enough, for example, or others are much better. All it takes is a gentle nudge from a trusted friend or colleague to set us on a better path.

Finally, ask yourself this simple question: what's the worst that can happen? The most common theme from all the interviews I conducted with leaders for this book was that they all asked themselves this very question. They mostly asked it when they found themselves stuck and avoiding action. They were able to realise the lack of action was often a result of a loss of confidence, no matter how momentary or long-standing.

Let go of perfection and your confidence will soar.

Comparison

Do you ever find yourself wondering why your performance is not as strong as that of your peers? Why others in your leadership team have much more influence than you? Why other parents seem to be juggling kids, career and life more easily than you?

When we make comparisons, we are actually comparing others' glossy outsides to our scruffy insides. Or as pastor and best-selling author Steven Furtick puts it, 'The reason we struggle with insecurity is because we compare our behind-the-scenes with everyone else's highlight reel.'

What people present to the outside world is usually an edited version of their reality. When someone asks you how you are doing, how often do you respond by saying, 'My husband is driving me crazy, I'm feeling like a failure at work, and I'm just about ready to lose my mind'? Instead, you probably bite your tongue and say, 'Things are really great!'

The study 'Misery has more company than people think: Underestimating the prevalence of others', published in the *Personality and Social Psychology Bulletin*, found that people tend to overestimate the presence of positivity in the lives of others, while at the same time misinterpreting or failing to detect negative feelings in others. So not only is what's being delivered an incomplete picture, we tend to distort the information we do receive – giving ourselves a double whammy.

According to what's known as 'social comparison theory', we compare ourselves with others in an attempt to make accurate evaluations of ourselves. But at what cost? While comparison can be a valuable source of motivation and growth, it can also spin us into a tail-chasing frenzy of self-doubt. Comparing ourselves to others hits us where it hurts in terms of our self-confidence. As 26th US President, Theodore Roosevelt, once said, 'Comparison is the thief of joy'.

Basing your worth on other people is disempowering. What others do is outside of your control and you can't change that. However, you can change the way you view yourself. Learn to stop comparing yourself to others to build your self-esteem.

And if you have a need to compare, make comparisons with yourself. Strive to be the best possible version of yourself, and make sure that you are continually learning and changing based on those lessons.

Compare how your performance is improving year on year rather than against all your other colleagues. Compare how bouncing back from a set-back this year took you less time than it did two years ago. Compare how much easier 'selling' that new program of work is for you now your influence has improved. Commit to growing a little bit each day, and celebrate the little advancements you are making without comparing them to those of others.

Fear

Fear tends to manifest itself as 'what ifs?' *What if I fail? What if people criticise me and my ideas? What if people reject me? What if I don't get what I want?*

This fear has a significant ability to negatively affect our confidence – like nothing else can. It is an emotion that overrides any rational thinking, can stop us from moving forwards and generally worsens our quality of life.

We often do not recognise the impact fear has on our confidence. We tell ourselves that we are anxious or stressed or worried about something, instead of using the words 'I'm afraid'.

In *The Confidence Code*, journalists Katty Kay and Claire Shipman define confidence as 'being prepared to fail'. I love this! Confidence is not about never feeling afraid or nervous or anxious. It is about not letting those feelings stop you.

I've already mentioned a colleague of mine Gabrielle Dolan – storytelling expert and author – in chapter 4. Even with all her experience, Dolan says that she sometimes gets nervous before getting on stage for a significant keynote speaking event. This is really surprising, and many people recognise Gabrielle as a very well-known and confident speaker. But, as she explains, 'who said confidence meant never feeling nervous?'

Self-confidence is not the absence of fear, but the mastery of fear.

As mentioned, fear is anything but rational. Sure, if we come across a snake in our path on a bush walk we are well within our rights to be fearful, but in a work context it's often an irrational fear that's holding us back – for example, we don't ask for a pay rise in case the answer is a flat 'no'. We don't put ourselves forward for promotion for fear we won't measure up against the other candidates.

This irrational fear restricts us, and means we never venture far from our comfort zone. It is what makes us avoid risks and play it too safe.

Stop and reflect

Instead of giving in to fear, ask yourself what one thing would you attempt to do if you knew you would be successful?

This simple question will turn the negative fear into a positive opportunity. For example, when I find myself procrastinating, I always ask, 'What are you afraid of, Michelle?' This is something I said to myself time and time again as I was writing this very book! Every time I sat down to write, I would quickly get up again and start cleaning the house or tidying the bookshelves. It wasn't until I asked myself this question – and realised I was afraid of failing or not writing anything good – that I could accept the fear and take action to build my confidence.

Remember, the most confident and successful people follow the cliché 'feel the fear and do it anyway' because they know that procrastination feeds fear while action cures it.

Face your fears

Here are some ideas to help you face your fears:

- ► Take a big picture view, instead of sweating the small stuff.
- ► Celebrate your small wins as you progress.
- ► Learn from what doesn't go so well, rather than beating yourself up over it.
- ► Put your own best foot forward; don't focus on what other people think.
- ► Remember what business psychologist Sharon Melnick says, 'It is better to put out a first iteration and constantly improve it with feedback than to not leave the gate at all.'
- ► Just start.

Overthinking

The following quote, commonly attributed to Mahatma Gandhi, and based on ancient Buddhist thinking, shows how powerful our thoughts really are:

> Your beliefs become your thoughts, your thoughts become your words, your words become your actions, your actions become your habits, your habits become your values, your values become your destiny.

Remember – research shows we have up to 70,000 thoughts a day. That is a massive amount of thinking! The way we think about ourselves, our abilities and our likelihood of success is a physical part of our brain. When we continue to reinforce those thoughts, whether they are positive or negative, we make that thought pattern in our brain stronger. Do you see how this can either build or destroy your confidence?

Overthinking and negative self-talk are two of the main culprits in destroying our confidence, and women especially are prone to overthinking. We think about work, the washing, what was said last night, whether we did that right, and what the weather will be tomorrow. Everyone is *always* thinking and it's impossible to turn off our minds completely. The tendency to overthink things, however, is a key differentiator between men and women, and why men seem to have more confidence than women in general.

Hillary Clinton was once on stage speaking at a conference for women. She was asked to give the younger generation some career advice. 'At this point in my career, I've employed so many young people,' Hillary began. 'One of the differences is that when I say to a young woman, "I want you to take on this additional responsibility", almost invariably she says, "Do you think I'm ready?" But when I ask a man, he goes, "How high, how fast, when do I start?"'

In *Men Are Like Waffles – Women Are Like Spaghetti*, relationship coaches and authors Bill and Pam Farrel expand on some of these differences between men and women. The Farrels use the metaphor that a man is like a waffle (each element of his life is in a separate box) while a woman is like spaghetti (everything in her life touches everything else). Men can literally think about one topic at a time – just the contents of one waffle square – and they can turn it on and off depending on which waffle square they are in. If they are in an empty waffle square, they aren't really thinking about anything!

Women, on the other hand, think like spaghetti. Every thought relates to every other thought; it's all intertwined. Something that happened to us this morning will affect us in the evening. We're not good at turning it off and sitting in empty squares.

I often hear from my clients who are challenged with their confidence that while they are waiting to voice an opinion or ask a question in a leadership meeting, the following thoughts are all going through their head at the same time: *Should I ask this question? Is it the right time for it? What if I look like an idiot? Maybe I should wait?* All of this while trying to follow the flow of the meeting – how exhausting!

It's important to pay attention to your self-talk before it spirals out of control, and both men and women need to learn to self-observe and pay attention to their thoughts. Managing overthinking is an important element of being able to step up with confidence – meaning this is not a gender issue but a leadership one.

Pay attention to your thoughts, and notice when they are positive. What has helped you be really positive? Also notice when they are negative or you're overthinking things. What has led to that? Identify the triggers or elements that are contributing to the negative self-talk or overthinking, and re-frame these thoughts to something more neutral or positive.

As I mention in chapter 5, one of the simplest tools I have seen clients use successfully over the years to change thinking patterns from negative to positive is mastering the art of gratitude. Making this part of your daily routine can train your brain to focus on the smaller (and bigger) things you are grateful for in life.

As outlined in chapter 5, a simple process is to ask yourself, and others, to identify the three things you are grateful for today. You can ask this simple question at the dinner table with your family, or before leaving work for the day with your team. With consistent focus on this, over time you will start to notice the good things in your day and your thoughts will start to shift to be more positive.

This kind of confidence can help you change careers, ask for more money, put your hand up for promotion and stop you hesitating and apologising.

Confidence turns thoughts into actions, so make your thoughts positive so they result in positive actions.

Overlooking possible role models

When Julia Gillard was first appointed prime minister, a red-haired daughter of my friend announced that she was going to be prime minister as well when she grew up. She said if Julia could do it, then so could she. This highlights that strong, positive role models help us to build our own belief and confidence because they show us how it can be done.

Role models are people who influence us by serving as examples. They are admired by us and we often emulate them. They can inspire us to strive without any direct instruction.

When these role models are confident leaders, they model how to exercise leadership effectively and confidently.

We need to look out for role models, because sometimes they are not obvious or right in front of us. Very often, we overlook the importance of role models in building and sustaining our confidence.

When I think back over my corporate career, I realise I had many people act as role models through the early and middle parts of my career; however, by the time I was in executive leadership roles, these positive role models were few and far between. So, when I was up against something or was feeling my confidence challenged, looking to role models to see a way forward wasn't easy.

Fast-forward to when I started my leadership business in 2012 and I made sure I had a number of brilliant role models around me. The difference this made to me taking action, developing myself and my business and, ultimately, building my confidence was amazing.

In many interviews, Madeline Albright has said that she never imagined that she would be the US Secretary of State. She'd been preceded by 63 male appointments and so had never seen a female role model in the position. In other words, seeing is believing, and imagining yourself being what you can't see is difficult.

Having role models can provide you with a filter for opinions that influence the impression you have of yourself. If you listen to the opinions of everyone and anyone around you,

you'll end up riding a confidence roller-coaster. You need to have positive role models whose opinions you value, and who will tell you what you *need* to hear, not necessarily what you *want* to hear.

Very often the only people you will listen to when given the *what you need to hear versus want to hear* feedback are these role models. You can see how they have been successful in the past so you understand this feedback is constructive and motivated by their desire to help you to be successful. On the other hand, positive role models can see what feedback might be important to you in supporting your confidence and helping you to step up.

The right role model will be someone who is more successful than you in terms of their career but, at the same time, is also similar to you in life. You need people around you who provide not only incentive and motivation, but also confidence and inspiration in terms of helping you believe you can actually become what you are trying to achieve.

Stop and reflect

Take a moment to think about your role models. Who do you admire and look up to? Who inspires you?

Remember, if you can see it, you can learn to do it! Don't overlook it. In fact, did you know that we can't recognise in others what we don't already have within ourselves? That means those skills or qualities just need consciously developing. That's a good sign for building confidence.

Your model self

To help uncover your model self, consider the following:

- ► Write down your top three role models. Who do you admire? Who impresses you?
- ► Who has been the most influential in your life over the last year, both personally and in your career?
- ► What is it about them that has affected you? What do you most admire about your role models and why? What can you learn from them?
- ► What are the qualities that you would like to emulate or have for yourself?
- ► What are five ways you could begin to bring some of those qualities into your everyday life?

Be aware and be you

Being aware of your own enemies of confidence is important. What is it that triggers a confidence hit for you? Knowing this about yourself brings you the ability to do something about it.

Be proactive about how you address your own enemies of confidence. They may poke their heads up now and again but once you know what you're dealing with and how to deal with it, your confidence will bounce back a whole lot quicker.

Be aware of your enemies, but always be you.

Check your confidence

1. What are your biggest enemies when it comes to building and sustaining confidence: perfection, comparison, fear, overthinking or overlooking?

2. Pick one area to work on first. What can you start doing more of to improve in this area, and to counteract your enemy? Once you have done this, move on to the next area, and so on. You may like to jot your answers down and refer back to them when you next see your enemies rear their ugly heads.

3. Who are your role models? What do you admire about them? What traits do they have that you can learn from or you would like to have yourself? Use the 'Your model self' exercise earlier in this chapter to help you realise how you might emulate those traits in your own life.

How was that? Looking your enemies in the face can be daunting. But it's something you need to do time and time again to really sustain your confidence and maximise your leadership potential. We'll look at other strategies to help you with this in chapter 7.

CHAPTER 7
SUSTAIN YOUR CONFIDENCE

I know what you're thinking. You've got to the second-last chapter of this book and I bet you're saying, 'Okay, Michelle, I can go away and apply these things to improve my confidence, but I've tried things like this before. They work for a little while and then here I am, back at the start. I'm back reading more strategies and books on how to improve my confidence.'

Like most of the leaders I work with, you may have already made real commitments to change and develop your confidence. You may have participated in training programs, read lots of self-improvement articles and worked on development plans. You can get things to shift for a little while but, eventually, you return to your old ways of working and thinking.

Why? Just what is going wrong? Is it a lack of skill, or something else entirely? As you've read in this book, building real confidence takes real work, and this work is hard because you're changing your *behaviour*. Look at people's New Year's resolutions as an example. Depending on the study, anywhere between 80 and 90 per cent of these goals (regardless of what they are) have been shown to fail within the first week. In fact, Professor John C. Norcross of University of Scranton Psychology, who for decades has studied resolution success and behaviour change, reports that fewer than 10 per cent of resolutions are actually ever achieved. Why? Because changing your behaviour is really hard! (For further thoughts from Norcross, see the article 'Solutions to resolution dilution', published by the American Psychological Association.)

Behaviour change is a well-researched area, and even instinctively we know that changing our behaviour in any sustained way is one of the hardest things any of us will ever try to do. Mostly, though, we don't know enough about why it is so hard, let alone what we can do about it.

Your challenge is to make those changes stick.
This is what will make your confidence sustainable.

Are you immune?

To make any kind of long-lasting change, you need to see that the benefits of engaging in the new behaviour far outweigh the outcomes from maintaining the old behaviour. You need to believe change is worth it.

The problem is we often have internal barriers working against us. Harvard Graduate School of Education professors Robert Kegan and Lisa Lahey call this 'Immunity to Change'.

In their book of the same name, they point to a study that found that when doctors tell heart patients they will die if they don't change their habits, only one in seven will be able to follow through successfully. If behavioural change is elusive for people even when they are faced with life or death choices, Kegan and Lahey conclude that desire and motivation alone can't be enough to change the status quo. Change remains maddeningly elusive.

The Immunity to Change work shows us that behind each of our habits is a strongly held belief that not only keeps us showing up in the way we do, but also works against any change that threatens the status quo. Kegan and Lahey liken this process to a finely tuned immune system because this resistance can be as strong, adaptive and systemic in us.

I love using the Immunity to Change process with clients who are working on building their confidence because it gets to the heart of what has been holding them back and makes a difference very quickly. The objective for you is to pinpoint and address whatever beliefs and assumptions are blocking you from the changes you want to make.

Mapping change

So just how does this process work? First, you have to develop what Kegan and Lahey call an 'Immunity to Change Map', which has four columns. From left to right, these columns are:

1. Improvement goal
2. Doing/not doing
3. Hidden/competing 'goal'
4. Big assumptions.

The following sections expand on the ideas within the map.

Clarify improvement goal

The Immunity to Change process starts by drawing up four columns to complete. In the first, you need to focus on outlining your improvement goal. This needs to relate to the behaviours you want to change to lift your confidence. (I imagine you will already have had many ideas as you have read through this book.)

This goal needs to be very specific, provide room for improvement and be very important to you. Once you have an idea of what this goal is, turn this into an affirmation statement and write it down. Examples of this include:

- 'I want to be speak up more in meetings and voice my opinion.'
- 'I want to be able to say no or challenge effectively when I have a different point of view.'
- 'I want to be able to negotiate my salary increase to a level where I feel valued.'

List behaviours

Next, uncover the behaviours that you are either doing or not doing that prevent progress towards your goal. Take a fearless inventory of these behaviours and record them in the second column.

This is about what you are actually doing or not doing behaviourally that works against your improvement goal. The more items you have here, the more honest you are being.

For example, if my improvement goal is to speak up more in meetings, I might list the following as working against this goal:

► 'I wait for others to speak before me.'
► 'I actively avoid going to meetings where I know I will have to speak.'
► 'I say no to speaking opportunities.'
► 'I stumble over my words and apologise before I speak.'
► 'I overthink what I am going to say before I can even say it.'

This exercise so far highlights your default model of change. However, if you just shine the light on your behaviours and try to reverse or do the opposite (as we would normally do when we attempt change), you will be in New Year's resolution mode. This doesn't work for adaptive challenges or the kind of behaviour change that is required to sustainably improve confidence.

Identify hidden or competing goals

Ultimately, you need to reveal your competing commitments or goals that are working against you, and so this stage is really important. When you get to this point in the map, you see what is really holding you back and preventing sustainable change.

This step is often the hardest because you're trying to take something that's usually invisible and make it visible. You do this in two steps, covered in the following sections.

Look at the behaviours you just listed

Consider your list of behaviours that prevent progress on your goals from column two. If you were to consider doing the opposite of each of these behaviours, what are the worries, fears or sense of loss that come up for you? You can record these fears and concerns in the top half of column three. This stage of the Immunity to Change process often feels really uncomfortable, but that's intentional – it's designed to be somewhat disruptive.

Continuing on from the speaking up example goal, some fears that might come up from doing the opposite include:

► 'I am worried I will be judged.'

► 'I am worried I will look stupid.'

► 'I am worried I will fail.'

Convert the worries into your hidden or competing goals/commitments.

Now turn the fear or worry into a commitment or goal to prevent this fear or loss from happening. Write this new commitment in the bottom half of column three.

For example:

- 'I'm worried I'll look stupid' becomes 'I am committed to not looking stupid'.
- 'I am worried I will be judged' becomes 'I am committed to never being judged'.
- 'I am worried I will fail' becomes 'I am committed to never failing'.

Surface your big assumptions

Big assumptions, like competing goals, are normally out of sight so, again, you need to make these visible as you complete the last step in the process.

Once you have begun to surface some possible big assumptions underlying your own immunity to change, you will be in a much better position to work on your immune system, rather than it holding you back either consciously or unconsciously.

Look at everything you listed in column three following the previous step and ask yourself, 'What assumptions must I be making to keep this true for me?'

What you will often find is that you are generally operating with one foot on the accelerator – the improvement goal – and the other foot on the brake. The competing commitments and big assumptions that keep your foot on the brake are typically unconscious. If you don't map them out, you can't address them to move forward.

Some examples of big assumptions include:

► 'I assume that others will add more value than I can by speaking up.'

► 'I assume that I need to have all the answers before I speak up (rather than asking great questions to uncover the answers).'

► 'I assume that if I speak up and it's not perfect, I'll be judged more negatively than if I didn't speak up at all.'

This tool provides insights you can use to make sustainable progress towards your goals, while helping you to dismantle limiting assumptions that are holding you back in life.

Mapping in action

To really understand how Immunity to Change works and how you can use it to help you build your confidence, let's work through an example.

Chris wants to be able to speak up in meetings and have a stronger voice. He's been told by his boss that he has real value to add, if only he could voice his opinion. Chris, however, finds this impossible. He always feels as if he will be judged when he speaks and so he stays quiet, especially if the topic is outside of his area of expertise.

When Chris looks at his behaviour using the Immunity of Change map, he sees so many things he is doing that are working against him speaking up. He:

► avoids going to meetings;

- ► doesn't prepare;
- ► only speaks about things he knows; and
- ► works himself up so that he is completely overthinking even one comment.

Chris has a fear of being judged and, ultimately, a fear of failure if he doesn't get things 100 per cent correct. This really holds him back. Exposing this helps him see that he will not easily speak up in meetings while he is committed to never being judged and never failing.

His big assumptions keep this fear alive. He assumes that when he speaks he won't come across as well as his peers, that other people can articulate ideas better than he can, and that being silent is better than speaking and getting it wrong.

So, how does he test those big assumptions? Chris might start speaking up in selective meetings and getting feedback from a trusted colleague. Chris can then see what happens. Did it really end in disaster? Was he judged negatively? Was it better for him to speak and have a point of view rather than not speak at all?

At each meeting Chris goes to, he can practise this more – he can try to speak up about things outside of his area of expertise, for example. The idea is to start with small experiments that are designed to succeed.

You don't want to start by testing an assumption that is so big and scary that you don't even try. In this example, Chris could try experimenting with different approaches in meetings and see what works best. That way, he can start to understand the assumptions that have held him back for so long are not so true any longer.

Once we can see our assumptions are false, we can move on from being captive to our immune system. Our improvement goal becomes easier to sustain.

Your confidence barometer

Our confidence generally goes up and down based on different environments, contexts and demands. And it can change depending on how we feel about ourselves and our ability. This is all pretty normal. Confidence is rarely in a completely level state, no matter how hard we try to sustain our behavioural changes.

Given confidence is a critical leadership skill, it is important that fluctuations in your confidence do not go unchecked. You need to regularly reflect on your confidence levels to give you a good indication of where a lack of confidence might be holding you back, or where a confidence boost is enabling you to step up and into something challenging.

Just as a mercury barometer acts to measure atmospheric pressure, a confidence barometer (shown in figure 7.1) acts as a simple visual tool you can use to measure your confidence levels.

Look at the barometer and ask yourself where your confidence is currently sitting. Is this where it usually sits? Is your confidence generally pretty stable? Or does it go up and down quite significantly?

You don't need to put an exact number on your barometer; instead, you can simply use it to give yourself some guidance as to whether you feel your confidence is at a low, medium or high level. The barometer is your visual reference, and a starting point for reflecting on your own confidence level at any point in time.

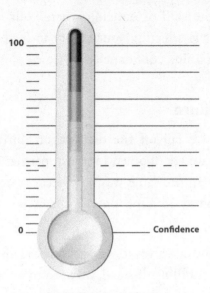

Figure 7.1: Confidence barometer

II **Stop and reflect**

Specific questions will help you reflect on what is positively and negatively impacting your confidence. For example:

► Where is your confidence when you are in your comfort zone and working with a group of colleagues you know well?

► What about when you are about to step on stage and deliver a presentation to a large group of employees for the first time?

Use the confidence barometer as a quick visual tool to reflect on your confidence in any situation.

Developing the skill of noticing where your confidence is at and how it is affecting your ability to lead effectively is crucial to sustaining confidence over time.

Embrace failure

Just because we fall off the diet wagon during a holiday doesn't mean we are doomed to return permanently to poor eating habits. In the same way, just because our confidence drops at a point in time doesn't mean we have lost all confidence.

When we allow ourselves to view relapse as failure, this often becomes self-fulfilling. Instead, we need to remind ourselves that failure is just an opportunity to learn.

Albert Einstein said that 'if you've never failed, you've never tried anything new'. Einstein's journey from a boy who some believe didn't speak until he was four years of age to the genius he is known as today took dedication, perseverance and a willingness to fail. This willingness to fail, to try new things and to view a relapse as simply that, will help you make change stick.

Never let a few days, or even weeks, of falling back into old habits and behaviours discourage you from re-establishing the behaviour you want to change. Instead, get back on the wagon and apply what you've learned in this chapter to support your behavioural change.

Check your confidence

1. Follow the four steps in the Immunity to Change Map: Clarify your improvement goal, list behaviours, identify hidden goals and make big assumptions. Use the exercise outlined in this chapter to help guide you through the steps.

2. Use the confidence barometer from this chapter to assess where your confidence is at right now. After meetings, events or presentations, revisit the barometer and see how your confidence has changed. Does it go up and down quite significantly according to different situations, or when you are out of your comfort zone? Or is it relatively stable?

3. What tips, tricks and techniques can you use from this book to help you regain your confidence at those times when it is low?

Congratulations, you are now well on your way to building and sustaining your confidence. What will you do first? You might try out some of your new skills in a meeting, presentation or negotiation with your manager. In any case, remember that your journey doesn't end here. I've provided one last tool that you can use to help you live life to your true potential. Read on to find out more.

CHAPTER 8
ASSESS YOUR CONFIDENCE

That brings us to the end of the book. But all the information and guidance I have given you will stay just a book until you start putting some of the things you've learned into practice.

So the first step to action is to assess where your confidence levels are at right now in the four areas we have covered in the book:

1. Show up
2. Stand up
3. Speak up
4. Step up.

The following Confidence Self-Assessment Tool will help you to identify which areas of your confidence are strong right now, and which areas require some development. You can then prioritise and target those areas appropriately through re-visiting the relevant chapters of the book.

The four elements in the confidence model each have four corresponding aspects to rate yourself on, and so determine your confidence levels overall. Along with rating yourself now, I suggest you chart your progress over time. When you complete this self-assessment tool at different times in your career, you can gain a sense of progress as you work to build your confidence. When you find your confidence dipping in a certain area, you can refer to the right chapter and do some of the exercises contained within to support you.

And remember – reflecting on the times when your confidence is high is equally important.

> *Reflecting back on how much progress you have made is helpful in building confidence in itself.*

The confidence self-assessment tool

Figure 8.1 again shows the four important aspects that make up my Real Confidence Model. The following sections take you through how you can assess your confidence in each of these four main areas.

How to use the self-assessment tool

In each of the four areas, rate yourself on the statements listed in the following sections using a scale of 0 to 10, where 0 is not at all and 10 is extremely likely.

Figure 8.1: The four main areas of the Leadership Confidence Model

Show up

1. I know what my greatest strengths are and leverage these in my leadership.

2. I am authentic and true to myself in the work that I do.

3. I look after my wellbeing and realise it is related to my energy levels.

4. I have a range of emotional management strategies in place that help me to bounce back from setbacks.

Stand up

5. I know what my values are and ensure I stay in alignment with them in all aspects of my life.

6. I am clear on my purpose and live my life in line with this.

7. I am deliberate about the responsibilities I take on at home as well as work.

8. I network with confident and optimistic people.

Speak up

9. I have a voice and speak up at a variety of different professional forums.

10. I use clear, assertive language in my interactions with colleagues, team members and senior leaders.

11. I am clear on the positive value I add and contribute well across different environments and contexts.

12. I use a variety of techniques to speak up and manage the impact I have with colleagues and teams.

Step up

13. I create a clear mental picture of myself performing well in demanding situations.

14. I understand that 'what got me here, won't get me there', and am optimistic about stepping up my performance and leadership.

15. I have a support network in place, including sponsors to support my career and growth.

16. I think proactively about the personal brand I need to create for myself that aligns to my future career aspirations.

Assess your scores

The following sections outline what actions you can take based on your responses in each of the four main areas of the Real Confidence Model.

Questions 1–4

If you scored 20 or below here, please refer to chapter 3 ('Show up') to gain guidance and learn suggested actions to build your confidence to show up as the best and most authentic version of you.

Questions 5–8

If you scored 20 or below here, please refer to chapter 4 ('Stand up') to gain guidance and learn suggested actions to build your confidence to stand up for your values, beliefs, teams and, ultimately, your leadership.

Questions 9–12

If you scored 20 or below here, please refer to chapter 5 ('Speak up') to gain guidance and learn suggested actions to build your confidence to find your voice and speak up to grow your influence and presence as a leader.

Questions 13–16

If you scored 20 or below here, please refer to chapter 6 ('Step up') to gain guidance and learn suggested actions to build your confidence and use strong, positive self-talk, build a personal brand that supports your career aspirations and have the sponsors in place to support you.

Check your confidence

1. If you haven't already, complete the self-assessment tool provided in this chapter now. Use your answers to determine which chapters of this book to revisit first.

2. Return and re-use the confidence self-assessment tool every quarter to see where you have improved and where you need to focus your energies next.

Above all else, remember that building and sustaining your confidence is a lifelong adventure. So enjoy!

DECIDING WHAT'S NEXT

After 28 years working in corporate roles, I decided to pursue my passion for leadership and start my own business. I've always had the self-belief that everything I try will turn out okay. After all, what's the worst that could happen?

So, six years ago, I made my dream a reality. But about one week before I left the security of my executive role, I felt like I was standing on the top of a building and about to jump off. *Oh my god, what have I done!* I thought. I hadn't even done any preparation for what was to come. My usual style was to 'wing it and see', but perhaps I was approaching this all wrong.

My confidence was low. I was confused. All sorts of questions ran through my mind: How do I start? What do I do now? What have I got to offer clients?

So the first thing I did was engage a couple of trusted colleagues for support and advice. I took advantage of some business mentoring to give me clarity and set me on the right track. I spent a lot of time reflecting on my own values and purpose and learned how to establish a business that I would love and would align to these values and purpose.

Once I started taking action, momentum grew and so did my confidence. I was pretty clear on my strengths and what I'm great at, so was able to leverage these strengths well. I was lucky to have a great network, and some of my best clients were the ones who reached out to me in those early days, trusted me and gave me work. I still work with all of them today.

It was action that gave me confidence. Step by step, I did the work to ensure I was showing up as the best version of myself every day – for myself and for my clients.

I did the work to understand my values and my purpose to ensure I was doing work that I liked with great clients. I found a different voice from the one I had as an executive, and worked to understand the impact I needed to have in this new context.

I worked on a positive mindset and self-talk, transformed my personal brand from executive leader to leadership expert and made sure I had the right sponsors in my corner.

In other words, I followed all the steps that you have just read through in this book. I applied all aspects of the Real Confidence Model. Still to this day, whenever my confidence is low on the barometer, I reflect on what I need to do to bounce back, and which areas I need to work on first.

*I am confident this works because it works for me,
and for so many others like you. All you have to do
now is act.*

Now you've read this book, you know what it takes to develop your real confidence. Plus, you know what is likely to hold you back. So it's now up to you to do the work from the inside out – this is the most sustainable way to achieve real confidence.

Every week I get emails or phone calls from people at all levels of all different types of organisations telling me their success stories. Here's just a small sample of the kind of feedback I receive:

- ► 'Michelle, I would never have put my hand up for this new role if you hadn't helped me develop my confidence.'
- ► 'Michelle, without developing my confidence, I would never have been able to deliver that major transformation program.'
- ► 'Michelle, without doing the work on my confidence, I would never have negotiated a pay that I am happy with.'

If you want to show up, stand up, speak up and step up with confidence, start today. I guarantee that once you start to act and make progress, your confidence will build. With sustained effort, your ability to lead with confidence will increase.

Remember, developing the ability to lead with confidence is not a 'nice-to-have'. Real confidence is your ultimate leadership skill.

Building and sustaining confidence is such a personal journey, but it's one you will never regret. I wish you all the very best on your journey to your leadership potential.

Michelle

CONNECT WITH ME

I receive emails and texts nearly every day from clients who have benefited from building their own real confidence. It is the best part of my day! So please feel free to get in touch – I would love for you to share your stories with me, including the trials and tribulations along with the wins.

You can find out more about me at my website (michellesales. com.au) and my blog is a great way for us to stay connected. If you need more one-on-one help, I run customised coaching programs and corporate leadership training. I can also speak at your event, so please contact me for more information.

My biggest love would be for you to share this book with your team, colleagues and friends. Remember, confidence breeds confidence, so the more you can do to help build confidence with everyone around you, the sooner we will all lift our performance and potential.

Contact me directly via michelle@michellesales.com.au.

SOURCES

Chapter 1

Dao, Francisco (2008), 'Without confidence, there is no leadership', Inc. www.inc.com/resources/leadership/articles/20080301/dao.html.

Kanter, Rosabeth M (2011), 'Cultivate a culture of confidence', *Harvard Business Review*. https://hbr.org/2011/04/column-cultivate-a-culture-of-confidence

Kay, Katty and Shipman, Claire (2014), *The Confidence Code*, Harper Business.

Chapter 2

Donovan, Maren Kate, *Escaping the 9 to 5* blog, http://www.escapingthe9to5.com.

Drucker, Peter (1967), *The Effective Executive: The Definitive Guide to Getting the Right Things Done*, Harper Business.

Eurich, Tasha (2018), 'What self-awareness really is (and how to cultivate it)', *Harvard Business Review*. https://hbr.org/2018/01/what-self-awareness-really-is-and-how-to-cultivate-it

Flaum, JP (2010), 'When it comes to business leadership, nice guys finish first', Green Peak Partners. http://greenpeakpartners.com/uploads/Green-Peak_Cornell-University-Study_What-predicts-success.pdf

Galliott, K (2017), 'View from the Top', *Qantas Spirit of Australia Magazine*.

George, Bill, Sims, Peter, McLean, Andrew, Mayer, Diana (2007). 'Discovering your authentic leadership', *Harvard Business Review*. https://hbr.org/2007/02/discovering-your-authentic-leadership

Goleman, Daniel (2016), *Primal Leadership: Realizing the Power of Emotional Intelligence*, Harvard Business Review Press.

Lyubomirsky, Sonja, Sheldon, KM, and Schkade, D (2005). 'Pursuing happiness: The architecture of sustainable change', *Review of General Psychology*, 9(2), 111–131. https://escholarship.org/uc/item/4v03h9gv

Rosenberg, Martha (2017), 'Interview with Brené Brown about Embracing Our Vulnerabilities', *The Epoch Times*. https://m.theepochtimes.com/interview-with-brene-brown-about-embracing-our-vulnerabilities_2339331.html

Chapter 3

Kranz, Gene (1967), 'The Kranz Dictum', NASA speech.

Morrison, Lieutenant General David (2013), video message about unacceptable behaviour. https://www.youtube.com/watch?v=QaqpoeVgr8U

Seligman, Martin (2006), *Learned Optimism: How to Change Your Mind and Your Life*, Vintage.

Chapter 4

Gallo, Carmine (2014), Talk Like TED: *The 9 Public-Speaking Secrets of the World's Top Minds*, Pan MacMillan.

Goleman, Daniel (2013), Focus: *The Hidden Driver of Excellence*, Harper Paperbacks.

Kabat-Zinn, Jon (1994), *Wherever You Go, There You Are: Mindfulness Meditation in Everyday Life*, Hachette Books.

Chapter 5

Anderson, Jane (2017), *Impact: How to Build Your Personal Brand for the Connection Economy*, Green and Gold Publishing.

Goldsmith, Marshall (2008), *What Got You Here Won't Get You There: How Successful People Become Even More Successful*, Profile Books.

Rogelberg, Steven, et al (2013), 'The executive mind: Leader self-talk, effectiveness and strain', *Journal of Managerial Psychology*.

Chapter 6

Dweck, C, et al. (2011), 'Misery has more company than people think: Underestimating the prevalence of others' negative emotions', *Personality and Social Psychology Bulletin*.

Farrel, Bill and Farrel, Pam (2001), *Men Are Like Waffles – Women Are Like Spaghetti*, Harvest House Publishers.

Kay, Katty and Shipman, Claire (2014), *The Confidence Code*, Harper Business.

Sullivan, Bob and Thompson, Hugh (2013), *The Plateau Effect: Getting from Stuck to Success*, Dutton.

Chapter 7

Dingfelder, Sadie (2004), 'Solutions to resolution dilution', *Monitor on Psychology*, American Psychological Association.

Kegan, Robert and Lahey, Lisa (2009) *Immunity to Change: How to Overcome It and Unlock the Potential in Yourself and Your Organization*, Harvard Business Review Press.

Notes

Notes

Notes

Notes